To My Son
Andrew Eastwick Longman

HOW TO READ PROVERBS

TREMPER LONGMAN III

IVP Academic
An Imprint of InterVarsity Press
Downers Grove, Illinois

InterVarsity Press
P.O. Box 1400, Downers Grove, IL 60515-1426
World Wide Web: www.ivpress.com
E-mail: mail@ivpress.com

InterVarsity Press® is the book-publishing division of InterVarsity Christian Fellowship/USA®, a student movement active on campus at hundreds of universities, colleges and schools of nursing in the United States of America, and a member movement of the International Fellowship of Evangelical Students. For information about local and regional activities, write Public Relations Dept., InterVarsity Christian Fellowship/USA, 6400 Schroeder Rd., P.O. Box 7895, Madison, WI 53707-7895, or visit the IVCF website at <www.intervarsity.org>.

Cover illustration: Roberta Polfus

ISBN-10: 0-87784-942-0
ISBN-13: 978-0-87784-942-1

Printed in the United States of America ∞

Library of Congress Cataloging-in-Publication Data

Longman, Tremper.
  How to read Proverbs/Tremper Longman III.
    v. cm
  Includes bibliographical references and index.
  Contents: pt. 1:1. Why read Proverbs?—2. Walking on the path of life
  —3. Woman wisdom or folly-which will it be?—4. What exactly is a
  proverb-and how does it work?—5. Are proverbs always true?—pt. 2:
  Reading Proverbs in context—6. Did Solomon know Amenemope and Ahiqar?
  : biblical proverbs and international wisdom—7. Proverbs in
  conversation with Job and Ecclesiastes—8. Proverbial wisdom in action
  : Joseph and Daniel—9. Where is God in Proverbs?: Christ, the
  treasure of God's wisdom—pt. 3: Following the themes in Proverbs—
  10. How to study themes in Proverbs: money matters—11. On loving the
  right woman—12 Wise words, foolish words—Conclusion: principles
  for reading the book of Proverbs.
  ISBN 0-87784-942-0 (pbk.: alk. paper)
  1. Bible. O.T. Proverbs—Criticism, interpretation, etc. I. Title.
  BS1465.52 .L66 2002
  223'.706—dc21

                                                                    2002012903

P 21 20 19 18 17 16 15 14 13 12 11 10 9

Y 21 20 19 18 17 16 15 14 13 12 11 10   .   .

CONTENTS

ACKNOWLEDGMENTS

Plans go wrong for lack of advice;
many advisers bring success. (Proverbs 15:22)

Writing a book feels like a solitary experience, but in actuality it is a community effort at every stage. I wish to give thanks to those who helped me write this book.

First, thanks go to my many students at various institutions where I have taught this material on the book of Proverbs. Most recently, I have lectured on Proverbs at Westminster Theological Seminary, Fuller Theological Seminary and Canadian Theological Seminary.

Second, I thank the anonymous reviewers of the prepublication manuscript, who made many helpful suggestions that they will find reflected in these pages. Even when I did not incorporate a suggested change, it helped me strengthen the case I sought to make. Of course, I relieve them of any responsibility if I made errors of fact or interpretation.

Dan Reid, my IVP editor and friend, offered comments that were of immense value to me. I thank him as well.

Finally, I again thank my family for their patience and support while I worked on this book. In particular, I have dedicated this book to Andrew Eastwick Longman, the youngest of our three sons. He will be heading off to Pepperdine University this year, and we will indeed miss his constant joyful and helpful presence. I will also miss watching him play soccer and lacrosse with such skill.

Tremper Longman
Summer 2002

1

UNDERSTANDING PROVERBS

■   ■   ■

ONE

WHY READ PROVERBS?

Life isn't easy. We may enjoy temporary rest from the battle, but no one is completely immune to the complexities of circumstances and relationships. These problems range from minor annoyances such as getting called to jury duty at an inconvenient moment, to major disasters such as a serious illness or a significant rupture in an intimate relationship. Sometimes we wake up in the morning and see the day as a series of obstacles to be avoided. We would love to be able to navigate life in a way that minimized the problems.

The Bible never suggests that the life of a follower of God will be devoid of problems. If anything, it says exactly the opposite. Life has its joys, but, according to 2 Corinthians 1:5 ("You can be sure that the more we suffer for Christ, the more God will shower us with his comfort through Christ"), even the joys are in the context of suffering. Unalloyed joy will come only in heaven. On this earth, we will have problems.

How do we handle life's problems? How do we deal with difficult people or uncomfortable situations? What do we say and how do we act? How do we express our emotions? The Bible has a word to describe the person who navigates life well; that word is "wise." A wise person lives life with boldness in spite of the inevitable difficulties.

But where do we find wisdom? We begin to answer this question by looking at the prologue to the book of Proverbs.

THE PURPOSE OF THE BOOK OF PROVERBS

The book of Proverbs leaves its readers in no doubt as to its purpose. After the superscription associating the book with Solomon,[1] the writer has a clear statement of its intention toward the reader:

> *Their purpose is to teach people wisdom and discipline,*
> *   to help them understand the insights of the wise.*
> *Their purpose is to teach people to live disciplined and successful lives,*
> *   to help them do what is right, just, and fair.*
> *These proverbs will give insight to the simple,*
> *   knowledge and discernment to the young.*
> *Let the wise listen to these proverbs and become even wiser.*
> *   Let those with understanding receive guidance*
> *by exploring the meaning in these proverbs and parables,*
> *the words of the wise and their riddles.*
> *Fear of the LORD is the foundation of true knowledge,*
> *   but fools despise wisdom and discipline. (Prov 1:2–7)*

TO TEACH WISDOM

At the very top of the list of the book's purposes is teaching the people wisdom. The words "wisdom" *(hokma)* and "wise" *(hakam)* run through the prologue and the rest of the book. To truly understand the book of Proverbs, it is important to understand this fundamental concept. Since the book's purpose, after all, is to make you, the reader, wise, it is clearly important to understand the nature of wisdom in order to benefit from reading the book.

Wisdom is a rich concept and is not easily summarized. We will develop our understanding of it as we proceed through the book. However, since we have to start somewhere, we will begin with the basic idea that wisdom is the skill of living. It is a practical knowledge that helps one know how to act and how to speak in different situations. Wisdom entails the ability to avoid problems, and the skill to handle them when they present themselves. Wisdom also includes the ability to interpret other people's speech and writing in order to react correctly to what they are saying to us.

Wisdom is not intelligence pure and simple. It does not necessarily exclude intelligence, but that is not the focus. Proverbs itself attributes wisdom to a series of animals, not because they have great intelligence but because they know how to navigate life well:

There are four things on earth that are small but unusually wise:
Ants—they aren't strong,
  but they store up food all summer.
Rock badgers—they aren't powerful,
  but they make their homes among the rocks.
Locusts—they have no king,
  but they march in formation.
Lizards—they are easy to catch,
  but they are found even in kings' palaces. (Prov 30:24–28)

These animals don't have a high I.Q., but the verses plainly describe a skill in living that is remarkable.

Speaking of I.Q., a recent book compares Intelligence Quotient to emotional intelligence.[2] The book, *Emotional Intelligence,* never once mentions the Bible or the book of Proverbs. But when the author, Daniel Goleman, describes the concept of emotional intelligence, it sounds very similar to the concept of wisdom in the book of Proverbs—at least at this initial stage of our definition.

People who have a high I.Q. know many facts; they can solve difficult mathematical equations. Their ability to reason and use logic is superior to others'. People with emotional intelligence have other abilities, including "self-control, zeal and persistence and the ability to motivate oneself."[3] They also have "abilities such as being able to motivate oneself and persist in the face of frustration; to control impulse and delay gratification; to regulate one's moods and keep distress from swamping the ability to think; to empathize and to hope."[4]

Biblical wisdom is much closer to the idea of emotional intelligence

than it is to Intelligence Quotient. Wisdom is a skill, a "knowing how"; it
is not raw intellect, a "knowing that." Goleman's remarkable conclusion
is that E.Q., not I.Q., correlates with success in life—success being the
ability to get and hold a good job, enjoy life and sustain healthy relationships.

Why read Proverbs, then? To gain wisdom, which is an ability to navigate life. We are, to be sure, just getting started in our understanding of
this idea of wisdom. We will see that it means much, much more than
how to make and keep friends or say the right word at the right time.
But that it does mean those things should contribute to our interest in
this book.

WISDOM'S COLLEAGUES

At the heart of the book of Proverbs stands wisdom, but this word is supported by a formidable collection of related ideas and words. As scholars
study the various words that are closely related to the Hebrew word for
"wisdom" (*hokma*), we get a fuller understanding of what wisdom is.

At this point, we won't discuss every word in the prologue that is associated with wisdom, but we will briefly mention those that most commonly occur, beginning with the word "discipline(d)," which also can be
translated "correction" (*musar*). This word indicates just how serious
wisdom is. Discipline/correction implies the threat of punishment or the
application of punishment if the instruction is not obeyed. This punishment can be verbal (Prov 12:1) or physical (Prov 13:24). It is the duty of
the teacher to apply such correction if the students disobey. Sometimes,
though, the punishment comes naturally on the person who takes the
wrong road.

The biblical word that is translated "successful" (from the Hebrew root
skl) can also mean "to have insight," and refers to a moment of recognition of the true nature of a situation. This recognition will allow the wise
person to act or speak in an appropriate way. Insight, therefore, is a key
element of a wise person's inventory, since, as we will see, a wise person
needs to read correctly not only the text but also the circumstances and
the people with whom the text is dealing.

Perhaps closest to wisdom in meaning, or at least the hardest for us to differentiate, are the words "understanding" *(bin)* and "knowledge" *(da'at)*. These words are used so many times that it is likely they are general terms. They may emphasize the knowledge or understanding of facts in a way that *hokma* does not. As mentioned above, *hokma* is not focused on intellectual knowledge, but the words "understanding" and "knowledge" remind us that such knowledge is an important aspect of wisdom. Not so, the idea of abstract knowledge or knowledge simply for knowledge's sake; that is not valued in the book of Proverbs. True knowledge is always for a purpose and in relationship with other people, God, or creation.

Discretion *(mezimma)* is another part of the arsenal of the wise. The word can also be understood as discernment, the ability to differentiate the right way to handle life from the wrong way. Prudence *('orma,* rendered "insight" in the NLT) is closely related. It describes one's ability to use reason to navigate the problems of life. Prudence carefully considers a situation before rushing in. It implies cool-headedness.

Finally, we turn to a group of words that reveals a crucial dimension of the idea of wisdom in the book of Proverbs. They describe actions that are right *(sedeq),* just *(mispat),* and fair *(mesarim).* These are ethical terms, and as we read on we will see that one cannot possess them without wisdom—nor wisdom without righteousness, justice and virtue. In other words, wisdom in Proverbs is an ethical quality. The wise are on the side of the good.

So, the prologue says in essence that the purpose of the book of Proverbs is to present wisdom, and the prologue's related vocabulary provides a rich picture of what it means to be wise. But we are still not done. The prologue applies these abilities in one special area, that of interpretation.[5]

THE ABILITY TO READ

The latter half of the prologue dwells on the ability of the wise person to interpret. Specifically, the following types of sayings are listed: maxims, proverbs, difficult sayings, words of the wise and enigmas. The exact translation and reference of some of these words are debated. For instance, many people understand the word translated as "guidance" (*tah bulot*) to be maxims, the word translated as "parable?" (*melisa*) to be difficult saying and the word translated as "riddles?" (*hidot*) to be enigma.[6] In spite of the quibbles over the exact meaning of these words, they all clearly represent Hebrew words that are difficult to understand not because they have a secret meaning or a code, but because they are forms of writing that address their subject indirectly rather than spelling it out in cold, factual language.

The book of Proverbs itself is full of difficult sayings and occasional enigmas. It is filled with imagery, which by its very nature is indirect language. In what way is wisdom like a "chain of honor" (1:9)? Who is Woman Wisdom? Indeed, we should point out that the Hebrew of Proverbs is much more difficult to understand and read than any English translation. Translations, after all, are really a commentary with no notes. Experts in Hebrew language and literature must make interpretive decisions in the very process of rendering the book into a modern language. Still, there are plenty of interpretive issues left when the work of translation is done.

Reading the book of Proverbs itself takes a skill that may be called wisdom, and the prologue dwells on the interpretation of writings. As we enter more fully into the book, we will see that an effective use of the book takes far more than an ability to simply read and understand the words on the page. The wise person is one who knows when and how to apply a particular proverb. Again, a full discussion awaits in a later chapter, but note the following:

> *A proverb in the mouth of a fool*
> *   is as useless as a paralyzed leg. (Prov 26:7)*
> *A proverb in the mouth of a fool*
> *   is like a thornbush brandished by a drunk. (Prov 26:9)*

Proverbs like these indicate that memorizing proverbs doesn't do the trick; in other words, mere knowledge of a proverb does not help a person navigate life well. There is nothing wrong with knowing the proverbs, to be sure, but such knowledge is not sufficient. After all,

Everyone enjoys a fitting reply;
   it is wonderful to say the right thing at the right time! (Prov 15:23)

Running throughout Proverbs and wisdom literature in general is the idea that proverbs are not universal truths that are always relevant and rightly applied; rather, they are context-sensitive. We will consider this idea later in the book, but for now, notice how it expands the scope of interpretation. Wise people know not only how to interpret the words on the page or the words spoken by other people but also how to interpret people themselves and, more broadly, the situation in which they find themselves.

Proverbs claims to be able to enhance our ability to interpret. Since all of life involves interpretation, this is no small claim.

TO WHOM IS THIS BOOK ADDRESSED?

The prologue identifies the book's intended audience. True, the discourses of the first nine chapters are addressed to a "son." That will be important to bear in mind as we try to understand the imagery in this initial part of the book. But the prologue is more inclusive and shows us that the final form of the book intends a broader audience for the whole.

As we explore the issue of the book's addressees, we observe that the prologue may be divided into three parts. The first part (Prov 1:2-3) is addressed to "people" in general. But the rest of the prologue, when divided into two parts, specifies narrower groups of readers. The first are the simpleminded, also referred to as the young (Prov 1:4). The simple *(peti)* are neither wise nor foolish. They are, in a sense, unformed. They can do stupid things, to be sure, and later in the book (e.g., Prov 1:22) will sometimes be grouped with the fool *(kesil)* or mocker *(lason)*. But the difference between the simpleminded and the fool or the mocker may be summed up in one word: teachability. Fools "despise wisdom and discipline" (Prov 1:7), but the simpleminded will listen. A modern word that describes the simpleminded in this context is "immature." The purpose of the book of Proverbs toward this group is to develop them as people along the right path.

The second specific group mentioned in the prologue is the wise or, maybe better, the mature. They too may benefit from the book. It will "increase teaching" and in particular enhance their interpretive ability.

In the final analysis, the book of Proverbs is for everyone—but with one notable exception. The fool is excluded. Perhaps it would be more accurate to say that fools exclude themselves. But why? The answer comes when we consider the final, climactic verse of the prologue.

THE FEAR OF THE LORD

The final verse of the prologue (Prov 1:7) gives what has been called the motto of the book: "The fear of the LORD is the beginning of knowledge." Later this will involve us in a more extensive discussion; for now we want to note that there is no wisdom without God. The wise must be open to God's foundational role in the world and in their lives. The fool is excluded because

only fools say in their hearts,
"There is no God." (Ps 14:1)

By definition, fools cannot participate in wisdom because they reject God. It is important, therefore, to begin with God. We do that by taking a close look at the leading metaphor of the first nine chapters: encountering Woman Wisdom on the path of life.

FOR FURTHER REFLECTION

1. The prologue to the book of Proverbs identifies three types of people: immature, mature, foolish. Where do you find yourself in that trio? Why?
2. What do you expect to find in the book of Proverbs? What are your goals in reading it?
3. Would you consider yourself intelligent? Wise? Both? Neither? On what grounds?
4. Can someone be smart without having a relationship with God? Can someone be wise?
5. Can you think of someone—a family member, a friend, a well-known person—you would characterize as wise? On what grounds?

FOR FURTHER READING

Estes, Daniel J. *Hear, My Son: Teaching and Learning in Proverbs 1-9.* Grand Rapids, Mich.: Eerdmans, 1998.

Fox, Michael V. *Proverbs 1-9.* Anchor Bible. Garden City, N.Y.: Doubleday, 2000.

Goleman, Daniel. *Emotional Intelligence.* New York: Bantam Books, 1995.

Kidner, Derek. *The Wisdom of Proverbs, Job and Ecclesiastes.* Downers Grove, Ill.: InterVarsity Press, 1985.

Rad, Gerhard von. *Wisdom in Israel.* Nashville: Abingdon, 1972.

Whybray, R. N. *Wisdom in Proverbs: The Concept of Wisdom in Proverbs 1-9.* Naperville, Ill.: A. R. Allenson, 1965.

TWO

WALKING ON THE
PATH OF LIFE

The book of Proverbs immediately brings to mind short sayings of practical advice on how to live life well. Certainly the book is full of such admonitions, prohibitions, and observations. (Later we will explore in detail how to read and apply this helpful material.) But the book of Proverbs is far from a random list of individual sayings, nor is it simply a book of practical advice.

To understand the book of Proverbs, we must first observe its overall structure. Admittedly this structure is not easy to see, especially if we read Proverbs with a hunt-and-find method—delving into the book as if it were a list of unconnected sayings, looking for those proverbs that are most relevant to our lives. We need to sit down and read the whole book from beginning to end without interruption.

But when we do, we will see the difference between Proverbs 1—9 and 10—31. While the latter contains individual proverbs, the former is a collection of lengthy discourses. We cannot be sure how many discourses are in Proverbs 1-9. Some have clear boundaries, with a change of speaker and an initial appeal for the son to pay attention. But the appeal can also appear in the middle of a speech, making it difficult to determine whether we are dealing with a new speech or a continuation of the old speech.

My best informed guess is that there are seventeen speeches, divided in the following manner:

Superscription (1:1)
1. *1:1-7: The Purpose of the Book*
2. *1:8-19: Avoid Evil Associations*
3. *1:20-33: Don't Resist Woman Wisdom*
4. *2:1-22: The Benefits of the Way of Wisdom*
5. *3:1-12: Trust in the Lord*
6. *3:13-20: Praising Wisdom*
7. *3:21-35: The Integrity of Wisdom*
8. *4:1-9: Embrace Wisdom!*
9. *4:10-19: Stay on the Right Path*
10. *4:20-27: Guard Your Heart*
11. *5:1-23: Avoid Promiscuous Women; Love Your Wife*
12. *6:1-19: Wisdom Admonitions: Loans, Laziness, Lying, and Other Topics*
13. *6:20-35: The Danger of Adultery*
14. *7:1-27: Avoid Promiscuous Women: Part II*
15. *8:1-36: Wisdom's Autobiography*
16. *9:1-6, 13-18: The Ultimate Encounter: Wisdom or Folly*
17. *9:7-12: Miscellaneous Wisdom Sayings*

I readily admit that these divisions are tentative; I set them out mostly for convenience of reference. In the final analysis, the number of discourses or where the divisions are made have no impact on our understanding of their content. In most discourses the father speaks to the son, but in a couple we hear another voice addressing the readers, a female voice (Prov 1:20-33; 8:1—9:17). We will soon see that this woman is at the heart of the message of the book of Proverbs.

LISTEN, MY SON . . .

Literary scholars have made us aware of a distinction between the implied reader/hearer of a text and the actual reader/hearer.[1] You and I are the actual readers as we open up the book of Proverbs at the beginning of the twenty-first century and seek to understand what it is saying to us. But we will never quite understand this unless we recognize that, in a very important sense, the book of Proverbs is not addressed to us. It is addressed to "the son." Throughout the book, the speaker of the discourses makes it clear that he is speaking to his son (Prov 1:8, 10, 15 and throughout). The speaker is identified as the father, and he is giving advice to his child about how to live life, avoid pitfalls and achieve success. We need to explore this literary dynamic to understand it more deeply.

The father/son dynamic is very common in wisdom texts, not just in Israel (see Eccles 12:12) but also in the literature of the surrounding nations. Later we will describe and comment on the relationship between the book of Proverbs and Egyptian literature; for now we will simply observe that all these ancient texts feature a father addressing his son. The oldest such text, the "Instructions of Hardedef," comes from the end of the third millennium B.C.—even before the time of Abraham—and opens like this: "Beginning of the Instruction made by the Hereditary Prince, Count, King's son, *for his son*, his nursling, whose name is Au-ib-re."[2]

Proverbs fits into this genre of literature; the teaching is of a father to a son. Is this a biological relationship or a master/apprentice relationship? After all, an older expert scribe would have described his disciples as his sons. For this reason, we can find a number of scholars who believe that in the book of Proverbs we have an older wise man speaking to his student, preparing him for his future career as a wisdom teacher in Israel.

There may be some truth to this understanding, since the book does contain a tremendous amount of material that is good advice for a budding young sage in the court. But that is not the entire picture. The book contains language and advice that stem most naturally from a family setting. Also, we get a subtle hint in Proverbs 1:8, where the father mentions the presence of the mother:

Listen, my child, when your father corrects you.
Don't neglect your mother's instruction.

Probably the best understanding, then, is that the book of Proverbs is a collection of wisdom sayings from different settings: the family, the court, and elsewhere. But wherever their origin, in their present setting they are addressed to the son. The implied reader/hearer, then, is a son, a young male. Realizing this helps us understand the nature of the advice given in the first part of the book and the impact of the imagery surrounding Woman Wisdom. To read this book correctly, we must put ourselves in the place of the original hearer, a young male.[3]

THE PATH . . . OF LIFE

One of the most pervasive metaphors of the first nine chapters is *derek*, a Hebrew term variously translated as "way," "path" or "road." Other Hebrew words are often translated similarly and used in parallel to *derek*, the more common term. This word occurs over twenty-five times in the discourses, and is implied throughout the whole section. For our purposes it will not be necessary to differentiate *derek* from its related words, since they are all building the same metaphor.

The path is a rich metaphor for one's actions in life. It implies a current point of origin (where you are in life now), a destination, and key transitional moments (forks in the road). In fact two paths are open to the son. The father warns the son of a path that is variously termed "crooked" (Prov 2:15) and "dark" (Prov 2:13). This is the path where dangers lurk, as Proverbs 2:12-15 shows:

> *Wisdom will save you from evil people,*
> *from those whose words are twisted.*
> *These men turn from the right way*
> *to walk down dark paths.*
> *They take pleasure in doing wrong,*
> *and they enjoy the twisted ways of evil.*
> *Their actions are crooked,*
> *and their ways are wrong.*

Another danger on this path is ambush by evil people. In the first discourse the father tells the son not to join such people in their attacks on others as they walk on the way:

> *My child (son), if sinners entice you,*
> *turn your back on them!*
> *They may say, "Come and join us.*

Let's hide and kill someone!
Just for fun, let's ambush the innocent!
Let's swallow them alive, like the grave,
let's swallow them whole, like those who go down to the pit of death.
Think of the great things we'll get!
We'll fill our houses with all the stuff we take.
Come, throw in your lot with us;
we'll share the loot."
Don't go alone with them, my son!
Stay far away from their paths. (Prov 1:10-15)

Other dangers include traps and snares that can foul up one's walk on the proper path of life. Indeed, though the dark path represents one's behavior in life, it does not lead to life at all but rather to death. We will explore this horrifying consequence at a later point.

The opposite of the evil, dark path is the right path, the path that leads to life in the fullest sense. Both the father and Wisdom urge the son to stay on this path. They threaten, warn, and reward the son so he will adopt this course of action. But the greatest incentive is that God is with those who are on the right path. He protects the path from the dangers that threaten to overwhelm the son:

For the LORD grants wisdom!
From his mouth come knowledge and understanding.
He grants a treasure of common sense to the honest.
He is a shield to those who walk with integrity.
He guards the paths of the just
and protects those who are faithful to him. (Prov 2:6-8)

In summary, Proverbs 1—9 teaches that there are two paths: one that is right and leads to life, and one that is wrong and leads to death. The son is walking the path of life, and the father and Wisdom are warning him of the dangers he will encounter as well as the encouragement he will find. We have named a number of both already: traps, snares, stumbling, enemies on the dark side; God on the side of life. But the most important people encountered along the way—and this explains why we need to understand that the addressee is a man—are two women: Woman Wisdom and the dark figure of Woman Folly. We will turn our attention first to Woman Wisdom.

FOR FURTHER REFLECTION

1. Why is a path a good metaphor for life?
2. How would you describe your life using the path metaphor?
3. Do you feel that your path in life has been basically straight or crooked? What makes it so?
4. Where is your path heading?

THREE

WOMAN WISDOM OR FOLLY—
WHICH WILL IT BE?

As we have seen, the path of life brings us into contact with many different people and decisions. None, however, is as profound as the encounter with Woman Wisdom. The metaphor of her desire to enter into an intimate relationship with the reader will have its strongest impact if we keep in mind—as already mentioned—that the implied reader of the book is male.

We first encounter Woman Wisdom in Proverbs 1:20-33, but she speaks most fully in chapter 8, a chapter that has captured the imagination of many readers down through the centuries. Those are the two places in the book where we hear Woman Wisdom speaking; the father describes her to his son throughout the first nine chapters. It is not always clear when the father is speaking of wisdom in the abstract, and when he is describing Woman Wisdom herself. But as we will see, the two are so closely entwined that such distinctions are of minimal importance to our understanding of the message of Proverbs.

Woman Wisdom is indeed a striking figure in the first nine chapters of the book, but she is not the only woman who meets the son on the path of life. Over against Woman Wisdom stands Woman Folly. She speaks only once, in Proverbs 9, and the father does not describe her at great length. But this woman also reaches out for a relationship with the son.

We need to understand Folly as well as Wisdom in order to recognize the dynamics of the book of Proverbs. (Two other women also appear: the wife and the "immoral" or "promiscuous" woman. We explore their significance in chapter eleven.)

THE ULTIMATE ENCOUNTER: WITH WHOM WILL WE DINE?

We begin at the end, that is, at Proverbs 9, the end of the first part of the book. We do this to better understand the significance of the detailed exploration of Wisdom and Folly that follows. Proverbs 9 presents a picture of the ultimate encounter of the young man with these two women, whom it purposefully compares and contrasts. The text is clear: he must choose between them.[1]

> *Wisdom has built her house;*
>   *she has carved its seven columns.*
> *She has prepared a great banquet,*
>   *mixed the wines,*
>   *and set the table.*
> *She has sent her servants to invite everyone to come.*
>   *She calls out from the heights overlooking the city.*
> *"Come in with me," she urges the simple.*
>   *To those who lack good judgment, she says,*
> *"Come, eat my food,*
>   *and drink the wine I have mixed.*
> *Leave your simple ways behind, and begin to live;*
>   *learn to use good judgment."*
> *Wisdom will multiply your days*
>   *and add years to your life. (Prov 9:1-6, 11)*

> *The woman named Folly is brash.*
>   *She is ignorant and doesn't know it.*
> *She sits in her doorway*
>   *on the heights overlooking the city.*
> *She calls out to men going by*
>   *who are minding their own business.*

"Come in with me," she urges the simple.
    To those who lack good judgment, she says,
"Stolen water is refreshing;
    food eaten in secret tastes the best!"
But little do they know that the dead are there.
    Her guests are in the depths of the grave." (Prov 9:13-18)

Here is the ultimate encounter on the path of life. The man is walking along and all of a sudden he sees two women, each described as speaking from the "heights overlooking the city." Each is issuing an invitation to the young men—an invitation to dine, an invitation to a relationship. We, reading the book hundreds of years later, find ourselves confronted by the same choice: Wisdom or Folly? Before we decide, we need to explore who these women are, what they are saying to us, and what the consequences of our decision might be.

WISDOM AND FOLLY: WHAT ARE THEY LIKE?

When we meet someone for the first time, we want to know what kind of person he or she is. The same is true if we haven't met the person but are talking to someone who has. The question that comes to mind is: "What is this person like?" The young man, who is the hearer/reader of Proverbs, encounters two women, Wisdom and Folly. Both reveal to him a bit about themselves. What do they say? How are they described?

We begin with Woman Wisdom. She is bold. We find her in the streets, the squares, the city gates (Prov 1:20-21). She shouts out from the hilltop near the road and at the crossroads (Prov 8:1-2). These are public places where crowds gather. She is not afraid of strangers. As we will see later, she carries an important message for them.

We know people by the company they keep and the people they avoid. Wisdom is closely associated with righteousness (Prov 8:6), truth (Prov 8:7), wholesome behavior (Prov 8:8) and good judgment (Prov 8:12); with common sense, success, insight and strength (Prov 8:14-15). On the other hand, she tells us that she stays as far away as possible from deception, evil, pride and arrogance (Prov 8:7-8, 13). Wisdom, then, is not just an intellectual category but is closely entwined with ethical behavior.

Particularly interesting is the role Wisdom plays at the time of creation. She claims that she is the firstborn of creation (Prov 8:22-26). She helped God create creation, indeed she calls herself the architect of creation (Prov 8:30). She rejoices with God and creation, particularly the human family (Prov 8:30-31).

Wisdom can have a dark side as well. She does not tolerate rejection.

I called you so often, but you wouldn't come.
I reached out to you, but you paid no attention.
You ignored my advice
and rejected the correction I offered.
So I will laugh when you are in trouble!
I will mock you when disaster overtakes you—
when calamity overtakes you like a storm,
when disaster engulfs you like a cyclone,
and anguish and distress overwhelm you. (Prov 1:24-27)

However, she offers significant reward for those who love and follow her, as we will soon see.

But first, what about Woman Folly? What do we know of her? Surprisingly little, as it turns out. Folly is described only in 9:13-18. Instead of being bold, she is brash (Prov 9:13); she sticks her nose in where it shouldn't be. She is ignorant, and worse yet, she is even ignorant of being ignorant. She is, as we will see later, the complete opposite of Wisdom.

TO WHOM ARE THEY SPEAKING?

According to Proverbs 9, Wisdom and Folly have the same audience: young men on the path of life. In other words, they address the same audience that the father does in his earlier speeches. But whereas Wisdom supports the message of the father, Folly seeks to undermine it. Indeed, throughout the speeches the father stresses that Wisdom is desirable.

The young men in the audience are described in a number of different ways. To Wisdom, they are simpletons (Prov 1:22; 9:4), mockers (Prov 1:22), those who lack good judgment (Prov 9:4)—fools (Prov 1:22; 8:5). She also calls them her sons (Prov 8:32). They are described as being on the path of life, but they are also the crowds at the city gate and other public places.

Folly, interestingly enough, has the same audience. Indeed, the first words each woman speaks—a call to the simple and those who lack good judgment—are exactly the same, as Proverbs 9:4 and 9:16 reveal. The men they beckon are immature, still in the process of development, and therefore at a critical moment of decision. Some are showing signs of resistance to Woman Wisdom: a simpleton, a mocker and a fool. Nonetheless, she still approaches, hoping to win them over.

As we read Proverbs today, we can see how—beneath the imagery—we are all part of the audience addressed by these two women. To read this book correctly, we must all—men and women, young and old—place ourselves in the position of that unformed audience. We need to make a decision: Follow Wisdom, or follow Folly.

WHAT IS THEIR MESSAGE?

Nowhere is the contrast between Wisdom and Folly more pronounced than in the content of their message. Both desire *relationship*—"Come in with me . . ." (Prov 9:4, 16)—and both have prepared a meal. Wisdom's meal is a sumptuous banquet in her magnificent house:

Wisdom has built her house;
   she has carved its seven columns.
She has prepared a great banquet,
   mixed the wines,
   and set the table. (Prov 9:1-2)

Folly has a more insidious meal in mind. She calls out to her listeners:

Stolen water is refreshing;
   food eaten in secret tastes the best! (Prov 9:17)

These passages are not allegorical, with hidden meanings behind such elements as the seven pillars or the wine. But they are developing a metaphor. In the ancient Near Eastern culture, to eat with someone is to form an intimate relationship with that person. These women want a relationship; because it is not possible to be united to both of them, they compete for attention. With which woman, reader, will you dine, Wisdom or Folly?

WHO ARE THEY, REALLY?

The text does not, of course, describe a literal Woman Wisdom or a literal Woman Folly. Who do these women stand for? The key is found in the location of their houses.

Let's begin with Wisdom. Her house is located in "the heights overlooking the city" (Prov 9:3). Indeed, the Hebrew text stresses that her house is at the highest point of the city. Here we need to transport ourselves back into the world of the original text, where we discover that the building on the high point of the city is the temple. This was true throughout the ancient Near East. Even the Mesopotamians, whose land was as flat as a pancake, built ziggurats, or stepped pyramids, human-made mountains where the gods were said to dwell. In Canaan, Baal was thought to reside on Mount Zaphon. In Israel, God appeared on Mount Sinai and instructed his people to build his earthly home, the temple, on Mount Zion.[2]

The location of her house makes clear that Woman Wisdom stands for God. She is a poetic personification of God's wisdom and represents God, as a part for the whole (synecdoche). Thus, the figure of Woman Wisdom fits in with a long list of other metaphors for God's relationship with his people, including warrior, shepherd, father, spouse, king and more. These metaphors point to the varied aspects of the divine character. We cannot reduce God to a warrior or a king or a shepherd or a father—or to Woman Wisdom. These are different manifestations of who God is for his people.

Woman Folly also has her house on the highest point of the city. When she calls to the men walking by, she is sitting "in her doorway on the heights overlooking the city." She too represents something other than herself: not the true God but the idols, the false gods and goddesses that tempted Israel away from Yahweh.

We cannot identify Folly with any particular deity. She could represent the gods of the Egyptians or the Mesopotamians. However, of all the gods of the ancient Near East, none were more alluring than the gods and goddesses of Canaan, at least according to the witness of the historical and prophetic books of the Old Testament. Most notably, there was the divine pair, Asherah and Baal.

When the Israelites entered the land, they encountered a people who worshiped these deities. The books of Joshua and Judges narrate how Israel displaced the Canaanites. However, from the very beginning, Israel found Baal, Asherah and the other Canaanite deities alluring. In the first place, it was common ancient Near Eastern theology that gods were territorial; some Israelites would have felt that to make things work in their new land, they had to appease the local gods and goddesses. Second, Israelite survival hinged on fertility, and Baal was a god of fertility. This meant that Baal was the power behind the rain and dew. With rainfall levels unreliable, famine was always a real possibility. In times of drought, then, the temptation to appeal to Baal for relief could be quite strong.

THE CHOICE

Proverbs 1—9 culminates in a choice that the reader must make before proceeding in the book. With whom will you dine, Woman Wisdom or Woman Folly? We now know that the choice is really between Yahweh and the false gods of the nations.[3]

To further understand this rich image, we need to consider more closely the ancient Near Eastern notion that to dine with someone is to enter into a deep and intimate relationship with that person. Indeed, the fact that it is a woman inviting a man to dinner resonates with sensual overtones. With which woman will the young man enter into a deep, intimate relationship? Proverbs makes clear that this decision is a matter of life or death—literally.

Take Folly for instance. Her meal is enticing, but notice what happened to her previous guests: "her former guests are now in the grave" (Prov 9:18). Baal and Asherah promised fertile fields and a fertile womb, both highly desirable. But the Israelites who thought they would receive life by worshiping these deities found death instead. That is the message in the Elijah narrative of 1 and 2 Kings, and in the warning of Jeremiah.

The setting for the Elijah narrative is the reign of Ahab, king of the northern kingdom of Israel. He has married a foreign princess named Jezebel, whose father was Ethbaal, the king of the Sidonians, a Baal-worshiping people. Ahab began to worship Baal (1 Kings 16:31), and Jezebel was a zealous evangelist for her god. Many Israelites turned away from exclusive worship of Yahweh and offered sacrifices to this foreign god, hoping for life-giving rains. But it wasn't Baal who was in charge of the rains—it was Yahweh. In response to their unfaithfulness, God raised up Elijah to communicate his message to Israel: "there will be no dew or rain during the next few years unless I give the word!" (1 Kings 17:1 NLT). Instead of life and crops, the worship of Baal brought death.

The prophet Jeremiah was raised up when the southern kingdom, Judah, was facing exile to Babylon. To confront Judah with its sin, the prophet spoke of her worship of Baal under the image of adultery. This is what he said about the consequences of following that lifeless god:

> Look all around you. Is there anywhere in the land where you have not been defiled by your adulteries? You sit like a prostitute beside the road waiting for a client. You sit alone like a nomad in the desert. You have polluted the land with your prostitution and wickedness. That is why even the spring rains have failed. For you are a prostitute and are completely unashamed. (Jer 3:2-3)

We are left in no confusion: following Folly (that is, worshiping Baal), though initially inviting, results in death—death in the form of drought (the spring rains have failed), and finally death in the form of the Babylonian army that destroyed Jerusalem and exiled the survivors (see the anguish expressed by the book of Lamentations).

To dine with Lady Wisdom, however, brings life. She herself warns that ignoring her message leads to death, but obeying it brings peace:

> For simpletons turn away from me—to death.
>   Fools are destroyed by their own complacency.
> But all who listen to me will live in peace,
>   untroubled by fear of harm. (Prov 1:32-33)

The father tells his son that a relationship with Wisdom brings great rewards:

> She offers you long life in her right hand,
>   and riches and honor in her left.
> She will guide you down delightful paths;
>   all her ways are satisfying.

Wisdom is a tree of life to those who embrace her;
  happy are those who hold her tightly. (Prov 3:16-18)

Notice the sexual overtones to the image of a deep and intimate relationship between Woman Wisdom and the male reader of the book. Such a person has really made wisdom an integral part of life. The result is like eating from the tree of life in the Garden of Eden, described in Genesis 2.

THE CROSSROADS

All of us who read Proverbs—even if we are a woman or an older man—find ourselves in the sandals of the young male reader, confronted by the decision whether we will embrace Woman Wisdom or Woman Folly. This is the ultimate decision of the book; it casts its long shadow over the rest of Proverbs, making all of the book deeply theological.

FOR FURTHER REFLECTION

1. Why do you think wisdom and folly are personified as women and not men?
2. Reflect on your life. What are three or four key choices you made that affect your present life?
3. As you consider these pivotal choices in your life, would you describe them as following Woman Wisdom or Woman Folly?
4. What kind of decisions are you facing at this point in your life? What would it mean to follow Woman Wisdom?

FOR FURTHER READING

Bostrom, Lennart. *The God of the Sages: The Portrayal of God in the Book of Proverbs.* Stockholm: Almqvist & Wiksell International, 1990.

Childs, Brevard S. "Proverbs." In *Introduction to the Old Testament as Scripture.* Philadelphia: Fortress, 1979.

Dillard, Raymond B., and Tremper Longman III. "Proverbs." In *An Introduction to the Old Testament.* Grand Rapids, Mich.: Zondervan, 1994.

FOUR

WHAT EXACTLY IS A PROVERB—
AND HOW DOES IT WORK?

Up to this point, we have focused on the first nine chapters of Proverbs. These lengthy discourses introduce the book and serve as a kind of interpretive guide to the second part, which is composed of much shorter and, for the most part, seemingly random sayings. It is these sayings that usually go by the name "proverb" and give the book as a whole its name. The proverb is the literary form that comes immediately to mind when we think of this biblical book. In the next few chapters, we turn our attention to this second part of the book in order to explore more deeply what is found there and how we are to interpret it. The previous chapters have set the stage, however, and we must not now lose sight of the relationship between the two major parts of Proverbs. In particular we must not forget the deeply theological nature of the pithy proverbs that we now explore.

WHAT IS A PROVERB?

The Hebrew word that we translate *proverb* (*masal*) has a wide application to many different kinds of literature. In this chapter, though, I use "proverb" to refer specifically to the short sayings that are collected in Proverbs 10—31. These are proverbs of a special kind. While we will soon see that there are many variations, I will start with a look at Proverbs 10:19:

Too much talk leads to sin.
  Be sensible and keep your mouth shut.

We are immediately confronted with the brevity of the saying. A proverb wastes no words. Proverbs are written in poetic form, and poetry in general is compact language. That is, poetry says a lot using a very few words. Later in this chapter, we will describe the poetic nature of proverbs more closely, but for now it is sufficient to take note of the brevity of these sayings. The New Living Translation does a good job here of preserving the proverb's terseness (the Hebrew has eight words, which the English translates with thirteen); sometimes a translation expands the number of words for the sake of coherence and clarity. The NIV, for instance, is even longer:

When words are many, sin is not absent,
  but he who holds his tongue is wise.

Thus, the proverb, and poetry in general, states its truths in as brief a form as possible. A lot of meaning is expressed in short compass. That is a signal to readers that they need to slow down and reflect on the meaning of the passage. A little later we will explore how to do this.

But what makes a proverb different from any other type of poetry? This, of course, brings in more issues than just its literary form. A proverb expresses an insight, observation, or advice that has been popularly accepted as a general truth. Indeed, a proverb can be so universally accepted as true that simply citing it is enough to end a conversation.

But notice this: a proverb is only accepted as true if applied at the right time. In chapter five, we will develop more fully the idea that proverbs are not intended to be universally true statements. We can see this, after all, in our own modern proverbs. Take the expression, "He who hesitates is lost." We can imagine all kinds of circumstances where this is true—and some people to whom we would love to say this with a sense of urgency. But there are other times when people need to hear the "contrary" proverbs: "Look before you leap" or "Haste makes waste." All of these proverbs are true—when applied to the right person or situation.

These English examples indicate another aspect of the proverb, also shared with poetry generally, that we often miss since we read the proverbs in translation. Notice the alliteration in "Look before you leap" and the balanced rhyme of "Haste makes waste." More than brevity characterizes these proverbs; they are often little literary gems, filled with poetic ornamentation.

With that in mind, let's consider some different aspects of the poetry of proverbs. We begin with the idea of parallelism, then imagery, and finally other poetic devices. This will help us understand how a proverb is put together by the author, so that we can read it for all its worth.

PARALLELISM

> *The king is pleased with words from righteous lips;*
> *he loves those who speak honestly. (Prov 16:13)*

The poetry of the Old Testament is largely constructed of parallel lines. Parallelism refers to the correspondence that occurs between the phrases of a poetic line. Notice in the above proverb the echoing effect that occurs between the two parts, or lines. (Scholars use the term *cola* to refer to two or more such lines and *colon* to refer to a single line; we will adopt that terminology here.) A rough, literal translation helps make the echo even clearer:

> *A king is pleased with righteous lips;*
> *he loves honest words.*

The verb "loves" echoes "is pleased"; the object "righteous lips" echoes "honest words." The explicit subject "king" is not repeated, but is understood as the antecedent of the verb in the second colon.

How are we to read the echo?[1] Our example shows that the relationship between the two cola is not mere repetition. The two cola are not "saying the same thing twice"—a common misunderstanding of parallelism. Instead, the second part sharpens and intensifies the thought of the first part. This is a general principle that applies to all parallel lines. As James Kugel, an important writer on parallelism, puts it, the relationship between the first two cola (labeled respectively "A" and "B") may be stated as "A, what's more, B."[2] B not only continues the thought of A, it also adds something to the message of the colon, frequently by focusing it more narrowly.

Take a look again at Proverbs 16:13. The first line says the king is pleased with righteous words; the second focuses on one particular type of righteous word, namely honest words. There is a sharpening of the idea in the second colon. This sharpening may take many forms; Proverbs 16:15 reads:

When the king smiles, there is life;
  his favor refreshes like a spring rain.

Again, we immediately notice the echo. Both cola comment on the effect of the king's favor, the second colon adding an image that reinforces the idea of the first. This is a different type of sharpening; the image communicates in a more vivid way than non-figurative language. We will have more to say about this in the next section.

The implication of our understanding of parallelism for reading the poetry of Proverbs and other portions of the Bible is to read slowly and reflectively. As we do so, we should ask, how does the second part of the parallel line contribute to the idea of the first part? If nothing else, such reading will get us to really concentrate on the meaning of the words. We may have a tendency to skim, but this does not work well, especially when we come to that compact language that we call poetry.

The previous example is similar to the vast majority of Proverbs in chapters 10—31, but we should point out that some parallel lines are longer than the typical two-part construction. Proverbs 25:4-5 show four cola that are intimately involved with one another:

Remove the impurities from silver,
  and the sterling will be ready for the silversmith.
Remove the wicked from the king's court,
  and his reign will be made secure by justice.

It is legitimate to ask whether to consider this a four-part parallel line or two related lines. But it is more important to recognize that these four lines are related to each other, with the first two cola providing an analogy from metallurgy for the point made about evil people in the second two cola. The repetition of the opening verb "remove" calls our attention to this. The wise person, working at court, will remove wicked people from the king's circle of influence so the reign will be just. This "political" measure should be carried out like the smelting of silver, getting rid of lead or other impurities in order to produce pure silver (sterling).

This proverb seems to come from the royal court and be directed toward young people who were entering royal service. Does the fact that most of today's societies have no monarch mean that this proverb is now irrelevant? Of course not. The principle still applies even if we are speaking of some other organization, say, a business.

PARALLELISM OF OPPOSITES

Before we leave the topic of parallelism, we should note that the book of Proverbs has a unique concentration of parallel lines that look at the same truth from opposite perspectives. This is called *antithetical parallelism*, and it involves opposites rather than similarities. This construction is found elsewhere in the Bible, but not with the intensity of the book of Proverbs, particularly in chapters 10-15.[3]

> *A wise woman builds her home,*
>   *but a foolish woman tears it down with her own hands.*
> *Those who follow the right path fear the LORD;*
>   *those who take the wrong path despise him.*
> *The proud talk of fools becomes a rod with which others beat them,*
>   *but the words of the wise keep them safe.*
> *An honest witness does not lie;*
>   *a false witness breathes lies. (Prov 14:1-3, 5)*

Each of these presents the same truth but from opposite perspectives. Though they are simple observations, there is no doubt about which side is being encouraged, even insisted upon. In regard to the third example, which would you prefer—being beaten with a rod or being kept safe? The implied message is to avoid the proud talk of fools.

Why is antithetical parallelism so prevalent in the book of Proverbs? As we have already seen, the book is intent on presenting its readers with a fundamental choice in life, the choice between wisdom and folly. These antithetical proverbs are fleshing out the differences between the two. Wisdom is constructive, demands fear of the Lord, avoids proud talk, and does not lie. Folly, on the other hand, is destructive, despises the Lord, brags, and lies. Antithetical parallelism supports the worldview and message of Proverbs as a whole.

BETTER-THAN PROVERBS

Another form that Proverbs uses to illuminate the fundamental choice between wisdom and folly is *better-than parallelism*:

> *Better to have little with fear from the LORD*
> *than to have great treasure with inner turmoil.*
> *A bowl of soup with someone you love*
> *is better than steak with someone you hate. (Prov 15:16-17)*

In the Hebrew, both these lines begin with the word translated "better." The English varies the word order a bit, but we can still recognize that better-than parallelism shows the relative value of two things. The comparison is between material possessions and the quality of relationships. Verse 16 says it is better to have a good relationship with the Lord and those near you than to have a lot of money. Verse 17 gets more specific, saying it's better to have a meager meal and a loving relationship than a hearty meal and a poor relationship.

The types of parallelism we have looked at occur frequently in Proverbs and provide a window into the overall message of the book. Other types need no explanation; they are easily understandable with the general principle of "A, what's more, B."

IMAGERY

Poetry is rich in images.[4] The book of Proverbs is certainly no exception. We already noted this when we studied the "mega-image" of the book, encountering Woman Wisdom on the path of life. But here we simply want to observe that we frequently meet images in the book.

What is an image (or symbol) anyway? An image compares two things that are essentially not alike. One part of the comparison is familiar, often something out of common experience; the other is less well known. The comparison seeks to illuminate the lesser known part. The dissimilarity draws our attention and gets us to look at something in a new light. This is the shock value of the comparison. Let's take a common image from the Psalms:

> The LORD is my shepherd;
> I have everything I need. (Ps 23:1)

Shepherds were common in the world of Psalm 23, and this metaphor invites a comparison between shepherds and the Lord in a way that will illuminate who the Lord is and how he acts toward us, his sheep. When we think about it, this comparison is shocking. In what way is the Lord of the universe like that smelly, cantankerous shepherd who lives near-by?[5] The psalm goes on to help us ferret out the similarity, and that is part of the power of imagery. It calls on the reader to unpack the image: In what way is X like Y?

Nowadays, the image of the Lord as a shepherd is so familiar that it has lost its shock value for most of us. If that is the case, then we should turn to Psalm 78:65:

> Then the LORD rose up as though waking from sleep,
> like a warrior aroused from a drunken stupor.

Now that still has shock value! In what way is the Lord like a drunk? The image captures our attention, and causes us to unpack the similarities among the differences.

We have already seen in Proverbs the rather shocking image for the Lord in the figure of Woman Wisdom. Now we will look at some local images like that in Proverbs 10:26:

> As vinegar to the teeth and smoke to the eyes,
> so is a sluggard to those who send him. (NIV)

Have you ever gotten smoke in your eyes? Most readers have. Maybe fewer have taken a gulp of vinegar and swirled it around in their mouth. But this image is asking us to reflect on that experience and compare it to sending a sluggard on a mission, in essence giving the sluggard some responsibility to represent us.

So how would you describe getting smoke in your eyes? I might use words like annoying, irritating, painful. Pure vinegar on the teeth? This is more difficult, if for no other reason than we don't know how ancient vinegar tasted. Perhaps we would use the same words as for smoke, throwing in bitterness as well. These words add punch to the idea that a sluggard will let you down, and this will have repercussions for your own reputation. The effect of the proverb is both to warn the simpleminded against being sluggards, and to tell the wise not to hire them.

I cited the more literal NIV translation as a tool for exploring the proverb. The NLT brings out the force of the comparison more explicitly:

Lazy people irritate their employers,
  like vinegar to the teeth or smoke in the eyes.

A final example of imagery is Proverbs 11:22:

A beautiful woman who lacks discretion
  is like a gold ring in a pig's snout.

That catches our attention; now what does it say? Basically that a lack of discretion spoils the appearance of a beautiful woman. The proverb encourages us to realize that discretion is an important value, more important certainly than physical beauty. Thus we should learn to be discrete, and avoid those who are not.

SECONDARY DEVICES

Parallelism and imagery—along with their companion, brevity (terseness)—are the most pervasive characteristics of Hebrew poetry. The ancient poets used many other tools to make their writings more intriguing,[6] so many that any attempt at a systematic survey of the devices used in the book of Proverbs would be fruitless. Anyway, most of them are hidden from the eyes of those who read the book in translation, and do not affect the interpretation of the text so much as they enliven the meaning and call for closer attention to the message.

This is true, for instance, in the case of the acrostic. Basically, an acrostic poem is one that starts each new line with a consecutive letter of the alphabet—in this case, the twenty-two letters of the Hebrew alphabet. Its purpose may be to assist in memorization, to communicate the idea that we are getting an A-to-Z picture, or both. In the book of Proverbs, the poem on the virtuous woman (Prov 31:10-31) is an acrostic. This poem, whose content we will explore in chapter eleven, is a full acrostic, each verse starting with a consecutive letter of the alphabet. There are variations on this theme, as in the most famous biblical example, Psalm 119. There, each eight-verse section consists of lines that begin with the same letter, followed by another eight-verse section that begins with the next letter.

Another secondary poetical device in Proverbs is alliteration: a sound play that creates coherence in a poetic unit and occasionally supports the meaning of a line. The Hebrew of the *bet* line in the virtuous woman acrostic (Prov 31:11) has a concentration of the letter *bet. Betah bah leb ba'lah wesalal lo' yehsar.*

One final example of a secondary poetical device in Proverbs is numerical parallelism. This follows an X—X+1 pattern, as seen in Proverbs 30:18-19:

> *There are three things that amaze me—*
> *   no, four things that I don't understand:*
> *how an eagle glides through the sky,*
> *   how a snake slithers on a rock,*
> *   how a ship navigates the ocean,*
> *   how a man loves a woman.*

Such a device is a way of saying that there are a number of different examples of the phenomenon, only a few of which are given. (The phenomenon here is the mysterious movement that leaves no trace, the fourth example being an allusion to sexual intercourse.) In Proverbs, the list that follows the introduction usually has the same number of elements as the second, larger number.

FOR FURTHER REFLECTION

1. Using Proverbs 21:14 and 14:20 as examples, define or describe the form of the proverb.
2. What advantages does the proverb form have for communicating the book's message?
3. How does the parallelism of 21:14 and 14:20 work?
4. How would you unpack the imagery of 14:27 and 16:24?

FOR FURTHER READING

Alter, Robert. *The Art of Biblical Poetry.* New York: Basic Books, 1985.

Kugel, James. *The Idea of Biblical Poetry: Parallelism and Its History.* New Haven, Conn.: Yale University Press, 1981.

Longman, Tremper, III. *How to Read the Psalms.* Downers Grove, Ill.: InterVarsity Press, 1988.

Ryken, Leland, James Wilhoit and Tremper Longman III., eds. *Dictionary of Biblical Imagery.* Downers Grove, Ill.: InterVarsity Press, 1998.

Watson, Wilfred G. E. *Classical Hebrew Poetry.* Sheffield, U.K.: JSOT Press, 1984.

FIVE

ARE PROVERBS
ALWAYS TRUE?

P roverbs 10:1 presents the first of the bits of advice offered in the second half of the book:

A wise child brings joy to a father;
a foolish child brings grief to a mother.

If we look closely and honestly at this proverb we will eventually question the "truth" of its observation. Is it really the case that a wise child brings joy to parents and vice versa? We can all think of many instances when we might question this assertion. Imagine an abusive, alcoholic father, or a self-absorbed mother who neglects her children. Are the lines of authority between parent and child so dominant that it does not matter what selfish, destructive impulses a parent has, the mother or father has to be pleased no matter what? Of course not.

It is clear that the father and mother are understood to be wise themselves. Their desires would be for the good of the child and for the furtherance of wisdom. This proverb is not insisting on an absolute law; it is rather putting forward a generally true principle that depends on the right time and circumstance.

A MATTER OF GENRE

Indeed, to read a proverb as if it were always true in every circumstance is to commit a serious error: we call it the error of genre misidentification. The proverb form, no matter the cultural background, presupposes the right circumstance for its proper application.

My grandmother was a veritable fountain of wisdom expressed in proverbs. As she prepared the turkey for Thanksgiving, she would say to my mother and my aunt, "Too many cooks spoil the broth." By this she meant "Leave me alone, the kitchen is too small, you will get in the way, I want to cook the turkey the right way, my way." However, after the meal, when we were all feeling sleepy and hardly able to move because of our full bellies, she would look at us and say, "Many hands make light work." The appropriate time had come for all of us to undertake clearing the table and washing, drying, and putting away the dishes, pots and pans.[1]

A CONTRADICTION?

We have records of a controversy among Jewish scholars of the Bible in the first century A.D. over the composition of the Bible. More specifically, there were some who questioned why five particular books were included among the authoritative, or canonical, books. Proverbs was one of the five. The nature of the controversy indicates that even at this relatively early age (though many centuries after the book was first written) some people had begun treating a proverb like a law.

The controversy centered on Proverbs 26:4-5:

> *Don't answer the foolish arguments of fools,*
>   *or you will become as foolish as they are.*
> *Be sure to answer the foolish arguments of fools,*
>   *or they will become wise in their own estimation.*

Some rabbis argued that these two proverbs were contradictory, and since God does not contradict himself or make an error, these two proverbs were an indication that the whole book was not canonical. Fortunately, this viewpoint did not prevail. Proverbs was already considered authoritative by most in the Jewish community at this time, and the doubts of a few did not change that opinion.

Indeed, both the proverbs are true if understood according to their intention, and the intention is signaled simply by the fact that these are proverbs. Proverbs are not universally valid. Their validity depends on the right time and the right circumstance.

THE RIGHT TIME AND THE RIGHT CIRCUMSTANCE

A wise person knows the right time and the right situation for the right proverb. Indeed, that is the prescription taught by the book of Proverbs itself:

> *Everyone enjoys a fitting reply;*
> *it is wonderful to say the right thing at the right time!* (Prov 15:23)

The wise person knows the right time to speak the right word, and the right time to apply a principle expressed by a proverb. Another wise man, Qohelet, often referred to as the Teacher or the Preacher, had this to say about the "right time":

> *There is a time for everything,*
> *a season for every activity under heaven.*
> *A time to be born and a time to die.*
>   *A time to plant and a time to harvest.*
> *A time to kill and a time to heal.*
>   *A time to tear down and a time to rebuild.*
> *A time to cry and a time to laugh.*
>   *A time to grieve and a time to dance.*
> *A time to scatter stones and a time to gather stones.*
>   *A time to embrace and a time to turn away.*
> *A time to search and a time to lose.*
>   *A time to keep and a time to throw away.*
> *A time to tear and a time to mend.*
>   *A time to be quiet and a time to speak up.*
> *A time to love and a time to hate.*
>   *A time for war and a time for peace.* (Eccles 3:1-8)

In a later chapter we will come back to Ecclesiastes and see that Qohelet has disturbing things to say about this truth, but for now we should notice that the wise person in Israel had a keen sense that there was a right time for everything, including the application of a proverb.

Proverbs are not magical words that if memorized and applied in a mechanical way automatically lead to success and happiness. Consider Proverbs 26:7 and 9:

> *A proverb in the mouth of a fool*
> *is as useless as a paralyzed leg.*
> *A proverb in the mouth of a fool*
> *is like a thornbush brandished by a drunk.*

These two proverbs say it takes a wise person to activate the teaching of a proverb correctly. A wise person is one who is sensitive to the right time and place. The fool applies a proverb heedless of its fitness for the situation. The two quoted proverbs are pointed in their imagery. A paralyzed leg does not help a person walk, so a proverb does not help a fool act wisely. According to the second saying, a fool's use of a proverb may be worse than ineffective, it may even be dangerous. Using a thornbush as a weapon would hurt the wielder as well as the one being struck.

So a proverb must be applied at the right time and in the right situation. The wise person is one who can do this effectively. But how does someone become wise?

THE ROAD TO WISDOM

How do we learn to read a person? How can we grow sensitive to the needs of a situation? The book of Proverbs recognizes a number of ways in which a person grows wise. They include observation, instruction, learning from mistakes and, finally and most important, the fear of the Lord.[2]

Observation and Experience. The wise person is one who has been observant in life. He or she has experienced a variety of circumstances and people and has learned from observation. Since experience is important to growth in wisdom, it was thought to be generally true that older people tended to be wiser than the young. As we will see later from Job and

Ecclesiastes, this certainly is not always true, but it is generally true. After all, in Proverbs 1—9 it is the father instructing the son, never the reverse.

Only rarely, however, does the teacher in Proverbs appeal directly to the process of observation in order to back up his teaching. Among those infrequent examples is Proverbs 6:6-8:

> *Take a lesson from the ants, you lazybones.*
> *Learn from their ways and become wise!*
> *Though they have no prince*
> *or governor or ruler to make them work,*
> *they labor hard all summer,*
> *gathering food for the winter.*

The teacher instructs his pupils about laziness by inviting them to go out and observe the diligent ant. From this experience, the teacher feels confident that the hearer will draw the lesson that follows in the text:

> *But you lazybones, how long will you sleep?*
> *When will you wake up?*
> *A little extra sleep, a little more slumber,*
> *a little folding of the hands to rest—*
> *then poverty will pounce on you like a bandit;*
> *scarcity will attack you like an armed robber.* (Prov 6:9-11)

Later, the sage warns his son about the dangers of an immoral woman by sharing the following observation:

> *While I was at the window of my house,*
> *looking through the curtain,*
> *I saw some naive young men,*
> *and one in particular who lacked common sense.*
> *He was crossing the street near the house of an immoral woman,*
> *strolling down the path by her house.* (Prov 7:6-8)

The story continues as it tells of the woman's seduction of the young man and the horrible consequences:

> *He followed her at once,*
> *like an ox going to the slaughter.*

He was like a stag caught in a trap,
    awaiting the arrow that would pierce its heart.
He was like a bird flying into a snare,
    little knowing it would cost him his life. (Prov 7:22-23)

From this observation the sage advises the son to avoid this woman (Prov 7:24-27).

Though this type of conscious reflection on the process of experience and observation is infrequent in the book of Proverbs, it does appear in more places than those just cited. Here are some brief utterances from chapters 10—31 that come straight out of a sensitive reading of people and circumstances:

Throw out the mocker, and fighting goes too.
    Quarrels and insults will disappear. (Prov 22:10)
Don't agree to guarantee another person's debt
    or put up security for someone else.
If you can't pay it,
    even your bed will be snatched from under you. (Prov 22:26-27)

Lazy people take food in their hand
    but don't even lift it to their mouth. (Prov 26:15)

Instruction Based on Tradition. Observation and experience allow the sensitive person to know how to navigate life. Strategies that succeed are repeated and taught; those that fail become the subject of warnings. The observation or experience need not be personal. We also rely on the learned analysis of others. Here, of course, we speak of the role of the father/teacher. In Proverbs 4, the father instructs his son based on the tradition handed down by his father:

For I, too, was once my father's son,
    tenderly loved as my mother's only child.
My father taught me,
"Take my words to heart.
    Follow my commands and you will live."

Indeed, we can also reflect back on Proverbs 7 in this context. The lesson about the seductive, immoral woman was based on wisdom gleaned through the observation of the father, but it was passed on to the son by instruction. The son did not have to directly observe or experience the situation to learn from it. In other words, we may learn wisdom from the traditions of others who have gone before us.

A new section of the book of Proverbs begins in 22:17 and is introduced by the following verses:

> *Listen to the words of the wise;*
>   *apply your heart to my instruction.*
> *For it is good to keep these sayings in your heart*
>   *and always ready on your lips.*
> *I am teaching you today—yes, you—*
>   *so you will trust in the LORD.*
> *I have written thirty sayings for you,*
>   *filled with advice and knowledge.*
> *In this way, you may know the truth*
>   *and bring an accurate report to those who sent you.* (Prov 22:17-21)

The thirty sayings represent a tradition passed from father to son down to the present time. From this instruction the son will grow wise. Indeed, that is the admonition of the following two proverbs:

> *The wise are glad to be instructed,*
>   *but babbling fools fall flat on their faces.* (Prov 10:8)

> *Get all the advice and instruction you can,*
>   *and you will be wise the rest of your life.* (Prov 19:20)

As we will see in the next chapter, Israel's sages depended not only on native Israelite tradition but also on the wisdom of the broader ancient Near East. In particular, we will examine the commonly accepted conclusion that the thirty sayings of Proverbs 22:20 have a special relationship with an Egyptian composition entitled *The Instruction of Amenemope.*

LEARNING FROM MISTAKES

Part of gaining wisdom by experience and observation is learning from one's mistakes. Proverbs supposes that everyone makes bad choices along the way. The difference between the wise person and the fool is that the former learns from mistakes and the latter simply refuses to change behavior. In this regard, the book of Proverbs uses two key words: *mûsār* and *tôkaḥat*. The NLT usually translates the first as "discipline" and the second as "correction." The two words are in the same semantic field (a group of words with related meaning) and often occur parallel to one another in the same verse.

Discipline and correction are directed toward those who wander off the right path, encouraging them to get back on. As it says in 12:1:

To learn, you must love discipline;
  it is stupid to hate correction.

And 10:17 states why it is good to love the one and hate the other:

People who accept discipline are on the pathway to life,
  but those who ignore correction will go astray.

Discipline is hard to accept; it means admitting having made a mistake. This is a humbling experience, but a wise person is a humble person, not a proud one. Indeed, Proverbs has a lot to say about the dangers of pride. In Proverbs 8:13, Woman Wisdom herself asserts how distant wisdom and pride are from one another:

I hate pride and arrogance,
  corruption and perverse speech.

On the other hand, God loves those who are humble:

The LORD mocks the mockers
  but is gracious to the humble. (Prov 3:34)

After all, pride has very negative side-effects and outcomes, while humility takes us back to the good path that leads to life.

Pride leads to disgrace,
  but with humility comes wisdom. (Prov 11:2)

Fear of the LORD teaches wisdom;
  humility precedes honor. (Prov 15:33)

Pride goes before destruction,
and haughtiness before a fall. (Prov 16:18)

So, learning from one's mistakes as well as observing the mistakes of others is an avenue to wisdom, which puts one on the road to life. Only humility, acknowledging one's weaknesses and failings, will allow this kind of instruction to work its benefits in one's life.

REVELATION: AT THE BOTTOM OF IT ALL

According to Proverbs, observation and experience, tradition and learning from mistakes are all important sources of human wisdom. However, at the heart of wisdom is God himself. Apart from God there is no true insight into the world. God is the only source of true wisdom. Even the ability to observe and experience come from the Lord:

Ears to hear and eyes to see—
both are gifts from the LORD. (Prov 20:12)

We have already seen that Proverbs establishes this from the very beginning, when it concludes its opening purpose statement with:

Fear of the LORD is the foundation of true knowledge,
but fools despise wisdom and discipline. (Prov 1:7)

The theme of the fear of the Lord reverberates through the whole book. After all, if wisdom depends on understanding the world correctly, how can that be achieved if one does not acknowledge that God himself is a fundamental part of the cosmos? Everything must be understood in relationship to Yahweh himself. This is what leads to humility, which comes, after all, from knowing that there is a greater power in the universe:

You can make many plans,
but the LORD's purpose will prevail. (Prov 19:21)

And so we look to the One greater than us to provide the instruction we need to navigate life:

We can make our own plans,
but the LORD gives the right answer. (Prov 16:1)

We have also looked closely at the figure of Woman Wisdom and have discovered that she ultimately stands for Yahweh. As we listen to her, we listen to God himself. Indeed, all true wisdom, knowledge, and insight, even that gained by tradition, instruction, experience, observation and correction, comes from God himself:

> For the LORD grants wisdom!
>   From his mouth come knowledge and understanding.
> He grants a treasure of common sense to the honest.
>   He is a shield to those who walk with integrity.
> He guards the paths of the just
>   and protects those who are faithful to him. (Prov 2:6-8)

WHAT KIND OF FOOL?

Wisdom, then, is not a matter of memorizing proverbs and applying them mechanically and absolutely. Wisdom is knowing the right time and the right circumstance to apply the right principle to the right person.

Returning to the "contradictory" proverbs about whether or not to answer a fool (Prov 26:4-5), we see now that the wise person must, to put it baldly, know what kind of fool he or she is dealing with. Is this a fool who will not learn and will simply sap time and energy from the wise person? If so, then don't bother answering. However, if this is a fool who can learn, and our not answering will lead to worse problems, then by all means, answer.

In a word, proverbs are principles that are generally true, not immutable laws. Bearing this in mind makes a world of difference when reading the proverbs. Someone reading Proverbs 23:13-14 from the New King James Bible, and having a mechanical view of the application of the proverbs, may well end up with a dangerous view of parenting:

> Do not withhold correction from a child,
> For if you beat him with a rod, he will not die.
> You shall beat him with a rod,
> And deliver his soul from hell. (NKJV)

Taken as a law, this would lead to parents beating their child out of fear that otherwise the child would end up in the fire and brimstone of hell. Indeed, a literalist would say that only a rod will do; that spanking with the hand is not permissible.

But this is not a law. It is a general principle that encourages those who are reluctant to use a form of discipline by telling them that it is permissible and even helpful for delivering a child from behavior that may result in premature death.[3] As with the fool in the earlier example, though, one must know what kind of child one is dealing with. Some children won't respond at all to physical punishment; indeed, it may hasten their path to the grave. Others may not need physical punishment but simply a strong reprimand. The key is that parents must know their child and the situation as they apply any proverb.

A PRINCIPLE FOR READING PROVERBS

Proverbs are situation-sensitive. We must not apply them mechanically or absolutely. Experience, observation, instruction, learning from mistakes and, most importantly, revelation—all these lay the groundwork for reading the text, reading people, and reading the situation. This understanding of Proverbs will become even more apparent in chapter seven, where we look at the gross misappropriation of wisdom sayings in the book of Job.

FOR FURTHER REFLECTION

1. In Proverbs, God's wisdom is mediated in four principal ways: observation based on experience, instruction founded on tradition, learning from mistakes and revelation. Read the following proverbs and categorize them according to those four categories: 23:9; 23:22-25; 25:1; 28:5.
2. Individual proverbs do not constitute universal law; their validity depends on the context. Read the following proverbs and consider how broad their application might be: 11:10; 12:10; 13:3; 14:24; 28:18.

FOR FURTHER READING

Brown, William P. *Character in Crisis: A Fresh Approach to Wisdom Literature in the Old Testament.* Grand Rapids, Mich.: Eerdmans, 1996.

Estes, Daniel J. *Hear, My Son: Teaching and Learning in Proverbs 1-9.* Grand Rapids, Mich.: Eerdmans, 1998.

Fontaine, Carole R. *Traditional Sayings in the Old Testament.* Sheffield, U.K.: Almond Press, 1982.

Kirschenblatt-Gimblett, Barbara. "Toward a Theory of Proverb Meaning." *Proverbium* 22 (1973): 823.

2

READING PROVERBS
IN CONTEXT

■   ■   ■

DID SOLOMON KNOW
AMENEMOPE AND AHIQAR?

Biblical Proverbs and International Wisdom

Though at first surprising, it should not unsettle us that the Bible is not a totally original book. Archaeologists have uncovered ancient writings from a number of cultures in the vicinity of Israel that have an uncanny similarity in form and content to the books of the Old Testament. Let me be quick to point out that there are always crucial differences in the midst of the similarities, but this should not make us turn our heads away from the similarities—especially when it comes to the wisdom literature of the Old Testament, and to Proverbs in particular.

After all, the Old Testament consciously places its wisdom literature squarely in the context of the wisdom literature of the ancient Near East. In 1 Kings, for instance, we have the story of God's gift of wisdom to Solomon. His tremendous wisdom is compared to the surrounding nations in the following manner:

> God gave Solomon great wisdom and understanding, and knowledge too vast to be measured. In fact, his wisdom exceeded that of all the wise men of the East and the wise men of Egypt. He was wiser than anyone else, including Ethan the Ezrahite and Heman, Calcol, and Darda—the sons of Mahol. His fame spread throughout all the surrounding nations. (1 Kings 4:29-31)

This passage does not disparage the wisdom of other nations; it simply says that Solomon's wisdom surpassed theirs. In and of itself, this encourages our examination of biblical wisdom in the light of the wisdom traditions of the surrounding nations. Accordingly, we will now look at the similarity between what we read in the book of Proverbs, and proverbs from the cultures of the Mesopotamians, Egyptians and Northwest Semitic people (particularly the Arameans). Not only will this help us understand better how proverbs functioned in ancient society, it will also uncover a place where the similarity is so close that it is possible that the Bible directly borrowed from its Egyptian source.[1]

MESOPOTAMIAN WISDOM

Sumerian literature. By Mesopotamia we refer to that cradle of ancient civilization that developed between the Tigris and Euphrates Rivers, with its southernmost base in what is now called the Persian (or Arabian) Gulf. Today this area is the country of Iraq, but at the dawn of history (c. 3000 B.C.) it was the home of the Sumerians. The Sumerians produced a very advanced culture, including the first known writing system, cuneiform, based on wedges impressed on soft clay tablets or chiseled on stone monuments. Except for a brief break, the Sumerians dominated Mesopotamia throughout the third millennium B.C. Among their writings is a significant wisdom literature, including a quite vibrant proverb literature.

Sumerian proverbs have been known to modern scholars for decades.[2] The evidence indicates that these proverb collections were produced in the context of scribal schools. Even the content of some of these proverbs shows the elitism of the learned sages:

> *A scribe who does not know Sumerian,*
> *what kind of scribe is he? (Sumerian Proverb Collection 2.47)*[3]

Bendt Alster summarizes the major topics of these proverbs as "a woman's daily routine, family relationships, the good man, the liar, legal proceedings, Fate, the palace, the temple and their gods, as well as historical and ethnic allusions."[4] In this list, we recognize topics of great interest to the biblical proverbs as well.

We can see, for instance, a similar concern with disobedient sons, and with recalcitrant wives:

A disorderly son, his mother should not have given birth to him. His god should not have created him. (Sumerian Proverb Collection 1.157)

A wise child brings joy to a father;
   a foolish child brings grief to a mother. (Prov 10:1)

A thriftless wife living in a house cannot eat. (Sumerian Proverb Collection 1.154)

It's better to live alone in a corner of an attic
   than with a quarrelsome wife in a lovely home. (Prov 21:9)

Additional similarities are evident regarding the dangers of promiscuous women. Consider these Sumerian proverbs, as compared with the lengthy admonitions found in Proverbs 5 and 7, especially 7:24-27.

Do not laugh with a girl who is married; the slander is strong.
My son, do not sit (alone) in a chamber with a woman who is married. (Shuruppak ll.33-34)

Do not have sexual intercourse with your slave girl; she will name you with disrespect (Shuruppak 1.49)

Do not buy a prostitute; she is the sharp edge of a sickle. (Shuruppak 1.154)[5]

And from Proverbs:

So listen to me, my sons,
   and pay attention to my words.
Don't let your hearts stray away toward her.
   Don't wander down her wayward path.
For she has been the ruin of many;
   many men have been her victims.
Her house is the road to the grave.
   Her bedroom is the den of death. (Prov 7:24-27)

Of course, we are dealing here, not with direct borrowing but with similar topics and attitudes. The biblical proverbs, even isolated from their context, are clearly not exactly the same expressions as the Sumerian ones. It is, however, more than a coincidence that these Sumerian proverbs, written down centuries before the biblical book of Proverbs, deal with the same subjects. Certainly the composers of Israelite proverbs were familiar with Sumerian examples.

Akkadian literature. During the third millennium B.C., there was a relatively brief time when Sumerian dominance was disrupted by an intrusion of Semitic people who have come to be known as Akkadians. Under Sargon the Great, they established rule over the native Sumerians for over a century (c. 2371-2230 B.C.). The Sumerians reasserted their political control, but this was short-lived; Akkadian-speaking people regained their ascendancy and held control of Mesopotamia for the next fifteen hundred years. Two major political powers during that time were Assyria in the north and Babylon in the south.

Archeologists have recovered many literary texts from ancient Assyria and Babylon. Creation texts (*Enuma Elish*), flood stories (*Gilgamesh* and *Atrahasis*) and others have evoked much discussion in terms of their relationship to biblical material. However, while there are Akkadian proverbs, they are not as numerous as those in Sumerian. Indeed, it may be that the Akkadian speakers were content with just the Sumerian proverbs. Nonetheless, there are extant bilingual proverbs (Sumerian and Akkadian) as well as two compositions, *Advice to a Prince* and *Counsels of Wisdom*, that, like Proverbs 1—9, have the form of a father giving advice to a son.[6] An Akkadian version of the *Instructions of Shuruppak* is also available. The Assyriologist W. G. Lambert speculates that Akkadian literature did not preserve proverbs in abundance because the Kassites (a group that intruded into Mesopotamian culture during the middle of the second millennium and played a role during that time in transmitting Akkadian literature) did not respect literature with oral or popular roots. For Lambert, this would include proverbial literature.[7]

EGYPTIAN WISDOM

When it comes to the background of the book of Proverbs, most attention has been placed on wisdom writings recovered from ancient Egypt. As noted at the beginning of this chapter, the Bible itself recognizes the wisdom of Egypt (1 Kings 4:29-31). Except for the Bible, no other ancient wisdom tradition has been studied so carefully.

The primary type of wisdom in Egypt goes by the native name *sbȳt*, usually translated "instruction" or "teaching."[8] These texts are often compared to the book of Proverbs and appear as early as the Egyptian Old Kingdom (c. 2715-2170 B.C.) and down to the Ptolemaic period (post-323 B.C.). It is one of the most popular genres in all Egyptian literature.

These "instructions" come mostly from the upper echelons of Egyptian society and deal mainly with advice about how to get along, and perhaps move up, in society. Their form is the now-familiar father who instructs his son. In some, the father is the king; in all, the father is old and experienced, about to step down from his high position in a society where the son is just starting. These compositions begin with a prologue that introduces the speaker and the addressee and often also states the intention of the text. Here is the opening to *Amenemope*—followed (for purposes of comparison) by the opening to Proverbs.

> *Beginning of the teaching for life,*
> *The instructions for well-being,*
> *Every rule for relations with elders,*
> *For conduct toward magistrates;*
> *Knowing how to answer one who speaks,*
> *To reply to one who sends a message.*
> *So as to direct him on the paths of life,*
> *To make him prosper upon earth;*
> *To let his heart enter its shrine,*
> *Steering clear of evil;*
> *To save him from the mouth of strangers,*
> *To let (him) be praised in the mouth of people.*
> *Made by the overseer of fields, experienced in his office,*
>
> *Who has a chapel at Abydos,*
> *Amenemope, the son of Kanakht,*
>
> *The justified in Ta-wer.*
> *[For] his son, the youngest of his children,*
> *Hor-em-maakher is his true name. (Amenemope I, 1-13, II, 10-13, III, 4)*

And from the book of Proverbs:

These are the proverbs of Solomon, David's son, king of Israel.

Their purpose is to teach people wisdom and discipline,
to help them understand the insights of the wise.
Their purpose is to teach people to live disciplined and successful lives,
to help them do what is right, just, and fair.
These proverbs will give insight to the simple,
knowledge and discernment to the young.
Let the wise listen to these proverbs and become even wiser.
Let those with understanding receive guidance
By exploring the meaning in these proverbs and parables,
the words of the wise and their riddles.
Fear of the LORD *is the foundation of true knowledge,*
but fools despise wisdom and discipline. (Prov 1:1-7)

This instruction genre is well attested; here are four examples: *Ptahhotep, Merikare, Amenemope* and *Ankhsheshonqy.*

Ptahhotep is the oldest of our examples—though not the oldest attested Egyptian instruction.[9] It is said to be named after the vizier under King Izezi of the Fifth Dynasty (c. 2494-2345 B.C.), but is generally understood to be pseudonymous and from the Sixth Dynasty (2345-2181 B.C.). It begins with a lengthy prologue, followed by thirty-seven chapters that constitute the instruction proper. The maxims promote the ideal of a quiet, contented man of humility, over against a heated, anxious, and striving man—similar to the division in Proverbs between the wise person and a fool.

If a son accepts what his father says, no project of his miscarries. He whom thou instructest as thy obedient son, who will stand well in the heart of the official, his speech is guided with respect to what has been said to him, one regarded as obedient. . . . (But) the induction of him who does not hearken miscarries. The wise man rises early in the morning to establish himself, (but) the fool rises early in the morning (only) to agitate himself. (Ptahhotep, 465ff.)

Merikare dates from around the Ninth (c. 2160-2130 B.C.) or Tenth Dynasty (2130-2040 B.C.), and is an example of a royal testament: the speaker is an unnamed king, and the one addressed is the royal prince. The king may be Achthoes III, Merikare's predecessor. But the succession of this time period is not completely clear.[10] A more likely explanation is that Merikare commissioned the text as a piece of political propaganda and placed the advice he wanted to follow in the mouth of his father and predecessor.

The *Amenemope Instruction* plays an important role in the interpretation of the book of Proverbs, which we will discuss shortly. Most scholars believe it was written in the thirteenth or twelfth century B.C.[11] The text is typical of Egyptian *(sbȳt):* Amen-em-ope, a senior Egyptian bureaucrat described as the "Overseer of Grains,"[12] addresses his son, Hor-em-maakheru. It is similar to other instructions in that it has an introduction comprised of a lengthy description of the speaker, a shorter one of his addressee, and a statement of purpose. The latter includes this description:

> *the teaching of life, the testimony for prosperity, all precepts for intercourse with elders, the rules for courtiers, to know how to return an answer to him who said it, and to direct a report to one who has sent him . . . , to rescue him from the mouth of the rabble, revered in the mouth of the people.[13]*

Amenemope is unique among the Egyptian instructions in that the advice section following the introduction is divided into thirty chapters, not the usual thirty-seven. The explicit setting and the advice all point to a court setting. Egyptologists have observed that this text signals a shift from previous instructions in that *Amenemope* values inward virtues and rewards more than materialistic ones. Like earlier instructions, however, it contrasts the "heated man" and his strivings with the humbler and more modest "silent man."

The final example is the *Instruction of Ankhsheshonqy* (sometimes transliterated as "Onkhsheshonqy").[14] The text begins with a narrative frame that explains why Anksheshonqy is writing a wisdom text to this son. In a word, he is imprisoned in connection with an attempt on the pharaoh's life, so he cannot teach his son personally. The prologue tells the events that led to his imprisonment: Ankhshshonqy, a priest of the sun god, was visiting his friend Harsiese, chief physician to the pharaoh, and got embroiled in a plot to do away with the ruler. The priest never joined the conspiracy, so he was spared a death sentence when the word got out. But he was imprisoned because he knew about the plot and did not report it.

Following this lengthy prologue is a large number of proverbs and maxims that make an observation or give advice. Their form is something of an innovation in that they are brief prose sentences. They have a random feel to them, though they are frequently grouped roughly by topic or form, and some themes are emphasized more than others. Given the prison setting of the advice, it is perhaps not surprising that one of the major themes has been described as "the ubiquity of change and the vicissitudes that go with it, and the fact that actions have consequences."[15] The following is illustrative:

When a man smells of myrrh, his wife is a cat before him.

When a man is suffering, his wife is a lioness before him.

Do not be afraid to do that in which you are right.

Do not commit theft; you will be found out.

Do not let your son marry a woman from another town, lest he be taken from you.[16]

Before leaving the Egyptian proverbial literature, we need to consider the concept of *Ma'at*, also personified as a goddess. *Ma'at* is hard to define, but it has certain affinities with the Hebrew concept of wisdom, particularly as personified in the person of Woman Wisdom. *Ma'at* is the harmony of the universe. It includes the ideas of order and justice. The instructions encourage the son/pupil in the direction of *Ma'at*, describing such a person as calm-headed or silent. The opposite is the heated person, anxious and striving. Again, similarities with the biblical categories of the wise person and the fool come to mind.

NORTHWEST SEMITIC PROVERBS

The designation "Northwest Semitic" refers to a family of languages that are closely related and were spoken during the Old Testament time in the area occupied today by Israel, Syria and Jordan. They include Hebrew,

Ugaritic, Aramaic, Eblaite, Moabite, Phoenician, Edomite and Ammonite. For all but the first three, only fragments of the language survive. In terms of nonbiblical proverbial literature, the only significant Northwest Semitic text is the *Ahiqar,* which consists of an interesting story, followed by a series of proverbs. The following summary of the story is based on the early fragmentary Aramaic text, supplemented by later versions.[17]

Ahiqar began his career as a counselor to the Assyrian king Sennacherib (704-681 B.C.). He had no son, so he raised his nephew Nadin to be his successor. After Sennacherib was murdered, Esarhaddon assumed the throne. Nadin betrayed his uncle, leading the king to order his officer Nabusumiskun to execute the older man. Fortunately for Ahiqar, he had once saved this officer's life, so he appealed to be spared. Nabusumiskun killed one of his eunuchs instead, and passed the body off as that of Ahiqar. Later, when the Egyptians approached Esarhaddon to request an advisor for a large building project, the king regretted that the brilliant Ahiqar was not available. Nabusumiskun chose this moment to bring Ahiqar back to public attention. He was greeted warmly by the king— then beat Nadin for his betrayal.

The wisdom sayings that follow this narrative are short and randomly organized, typical of most proverbial collections, including those in Proverbs. In the following examples, the first resembles the form of the numerical proverbs found in the biblical book (for example, Proverbs 6:16-19); the second recalls the content of Proverbs 23:13-14, which recommends the rod for punishment.

> *There are two things which are good,*
> *and a third which is pleasing to Samas;*
> *one who drinks wine and shares it,*
> *one who masters wisdom [and observes it;]*
> *and one who hears a word but tells it not.*
> *Now that is precious to Samas.*
> *(Saying 12)*
>
> *Spare not your son from the rod; otherwise, can you save him [from wickedness]?*
> *(Saying 3)*

IMPLICATIONS

As noted earlier, 1 Kings 4 points to an international context for Israel's wisdom literature. Having surveyed some highpoints of Egyptian, Sumerian, Akkadian and Northwest Semitic proverb literature, we see how studying Hebrew wisdom in the light of the broader ancient Near East can give us a much deeper understanding of the texts. In all traditions, wisdom is not abstract and philosophical but practical, with the hope of getting on in life.[18] The following are a few notable examples of illuminating comparisons.

Father-Son. All the surveyed cultures of the ancient Near East evidence proverb literature in which a father addresses his son. In the prologues of the Egyptian Instruction texts the father and the son are named, but this father-son dynamic is not always carried forward into the advice section. (In this regard, the book of Proverbs is most like *Ahiqar*, which is not surprising because that Aramaic text is closer culturally to the book of Proverbs.) This characteristic of the Egyptian literature has been used to argue that the father-son relationship is professional, not biological: a master is addressing his pupil or apprentice, the one who will follow him in his career. But this does not negate the likelihood that a biological son would also follow his father into his career. Both the biological and the professional interpretations may well be true.

In any case, the book of Proverbs expresses both professional interests (etiquette before the king, for example) and familial concerns. Furthermore, it includes instruction not only from the father but from the mother as well (Prov 1:8; 6:20; 31:1). This makes a purely professional interpretation difficult to maintain.

Amenemope and Proverbs. Perhaps the most celebrated comparison is that between Proverbs 22:17—24:22 and the Egyptian Instruction *Amenemope*, described above. When this text came to the attention of the scholarly world in the 1920s, it launched a discussion of the relationship between biblical wisdom and Egyptian wisdom that has lasted to the present day. Though debate continues over the exact nature of that relationship, it is impossible to deny that similarities exist between *Amenemope* and the "sayings of the wise" section of the biblical book of Proverbs

(Prov 22:17—24:22). But other similarities fall outside that section of Proverbs, as the following examples demonstrate:[19]

> *Don't rob the poor just because you can,*
> *   or exploit the needy in court. (Prov 22:22)*

> *Guard yourself from robbing the poor*
> *From being violent to the weak. (Amenemope IV, 4-5)*

> *Do you see any truly competent workers?*
> *   They will serve kings*
> *   rather than ordinary people. (Prov 22:29)*

> *As for the scribe who is experienced in his office*
> *He will find himself worthy to be a courtier. (Amenemope XXVII, 16-17)*

> *Don't wear yourself out trying to get rich.*
> *   Be wise enough to know when to quit.*
> *Just blink your eyes and wealth is gone,*
> *   for it will sprout wings*
> *   and fly away like an eagle. (Prov 23:4-5)*

> *Do not strain to seek excess*
> *When your possessions are secure*
> *If riches are brought to you by robbery*
> *They will not stay the night in your possession*
> *When the day dawns they are no longer in your house.*
> *Their place can be seen but they are no longer there*
> *The earth opened its mouth to crush and swallow them*
> *And plunged them to Dust.*
> *They make themselves a great hole, as large as they are.*
> *And sink themselves in the underworld.*
> *They make themselves wings like geese,*
> *And fly to heaven. (Amenemope IX, 14—x, 5)*

> *Don't cheat your neighbor by moving the ancient boundary markers;*
> *   don't take the land of defenseless orphans.*
> *For their Redeemer is strong;*
> *   he himself will bring their charges against you. (Prov 23:10-11)*

Do not remove the boundary stone of the cultivated land.
Nor throw down the boundary of the widow. (Amenemope VII, 12)

These and other parallels have led to an intense debate over the origin of the wisdom reflected in both texts. Advocates may be cited for Egyptian priority,[20] Israelite priority[21] and a third common source. One difficulty in resolving this question is the uncertainty over when parts of Proverbs were written—or, for that matter, when *Amenemope* was written. The fact that a problematic word in Proverbs 22:20 can easily be interpreted to mean "thirty," and *Amenemope* has thirty sayings, has led most modern translations (NRSV, NIV, NLT) to make the following emendation in the biblical text:

I have written thirty sayings for you,
  filled with advice and knowledge.[22]

Some scholars argue that the similarities between *Amenemope* and Proverbs are not unique, that the more we learn about Egyptian instruction the more parallels we will see not only with this one text but with many others. We also see similarities between the wisdom ideas of *Amenemope* and Proverbs, and the wisdom of other cultures, most notably the Aramaic *Ahiqar*. Perhaps the best conclusion is that there is not a specific relationship between Proverbs and *Amenemope*, but both texts are part of an international tradition of wisdom that shares many similarities. In the light of those similarities, the differences in Proverbs—particularly the connection between Yahweh and wisdom—stand out even more.

WISDOM THEMES

We cannot help but be struck by the similar interests and themes that appear in the wisdom of the cultures of the ancient Near East. Indeed, as we have already seen in *Amenemope* and Proverbs 22:17—24:12 that there are even some specific connections between individual proverbs.

The dangerous woman. Wisdom traditions from Egypt, Mesopotamia and Palestine all warn their young male readers of the dangers of the promiscuous woman, or of taking up with a married woman. It is not good for one's career or for one's health—especially taking into account the anger of a jealous husband. Such a relationship would also lead the young man into crazy actions and distract him from his own family. This is a major theme in Proverbs, particularly the first nine chapters, and may be illustrated by Proverbs 6:23-26:

> *For their command is a lamp*
>   *and their instruction a light;*
> *Their corrective discipline*
>   *is the way to life.*
> *It will keep you from the immoral woman,*
>   *from the smooth tongue of the promiscuous woman.*
> *Don't lust for her beauty,*
>   *don't let her coy glances seduce you.*
> *For a prostitute will bring you to poverty,*
>   *but sleeping with another man's wife will cost you your life.*

Compare that with the following passages from other Near Eastern wisdom texts:

> *Don't marry a prostitute, whose husbands are legion,*
> *Nor a temple harlot, who is dedicated to a goddess,*
> *Nor a courtesan, whose intimates are numerous.*
> *She will not sustain you in your time of trouble,*
> *She will snigger at you when you are embroiled in controversy.*
> *She has neither respect nor obedience in her nature.*
> *Even if she has the run of your house, get rid of her,*
> *She has ears attuned for another's footfall. (Akkadian Counsels of Wisdom)*[23]

> *Take a wife while you're young,*
> *That she make a son for you;*
> *She should bear for you while you're youthful,*
> *It is proper to make people.*

> *Beware of a woman who is a stranger.*
> *One not known in her town;*
> *Don't stare at her when she goes by,*
> *Do not know her carnally.*
> *A deep water whose course is unknown,*

Such a woman away from her husband.
"I am pretty," she tells you daily,
when she has no witnesses;
she is ready to ensnare you,
a great deadly crime when it is heard. (Egyptian Instructions of Ani)[24]

The wise and the fool. The nature of an instruction presumes that there is a right way and a wrong way to live. All the ancient Near Eastern traditions underline this and provide advice about how to navigate life in a way that minimizes trouble and maximizes success. In Proverbs, the ideal is the wise person, and wisdom connects with righteousness, an ethical category. In Egyptian literature, the ideal is the cool-headed or silent person, while the opposite category is the heated person. While the cool-headed person is calm and acts according to the circumstances, the heated person is anxious, pushy, inappropriately emotional. Though there are differences, the biblical and the Egyptian categories overlap.

Do not befriend the heated man,
Nor approach him for conversation. (Amenemope chapter 9)

Don't answer the foolish arguments of fools,
or you will become as foolish as they are. (Prov 26:4)

There are other similarities between the biblical polarities of wise and foolish people and the Egyptian contrast of the heated and cool person, but there is also a major difference. In its broader context, wisdom in Proverbs is a deeply theological concept. If one is wise, then one is in relationship with Woman Wisdom—who is Yahweh's wisdom personified—and ultimately with Yahweh himself. Egyptian wisdom is certainly not secular: *Ma'at*, after all, is the central concept, is upheld by the gods, and at times is personified as a goddess. But the Egyptian instructions are not as ostensibly religious.

Etiquette before the king. Much of the advice of ancient Near Eastern wisdom is directed toward young courtiers who are destined to serve in the royal court. This is true of Proverbs as well, though we have already seen that it collects wisdom from many settings, not just the court. A few citations, though, show that Egyptian and biblical wisdom share an interest in something as seemingly down-to-earth as table manners:

> *When you are guest at the table of one who is greater than you then take what he gives you, as they serve it before you. Do not look at what lies before him, but always look only at what lies before you. (Ptahhotep)*

> *Do not eat in the presence of an official and then set your mouth before (him). If you are sated pretend to chew. Content yourself with your saliva. Look at the bowl that is before you, and let it serve your needs. An official is great in his office, as well as rich in drawings of water. (Amenemope xxiii, 13-20)*

> *While dining with a ruler,*
>   *pay attention to what is put before you.*
> *If you are a big eater,*
>   *put a knife to your throat;*
> *and don't desire all the delicacies,*
>   *for he might be trying to fool you. (Prov 23:1-3)*

Other similar topics. We have already seen similar proverbs in *Amenemope* and the biblical book of Proverbs. Such parallels are not restricted to these two works, but include the works of other Near Eastern cultures. By way of illustration, note the similar admonition about overdrinking in the *Instruction of Ani* and in Proverbs:

> *Don't indulge in drinking beer,*
> *Lest you utter evil speech*
> *And don't know what you're saying. (Ani)*

> *Wine produces mockers; liquor leads to brawls.*
>   *Those led astray by drink cannot be wise. (Prov 20:1; see also 31:4-5)*

WISDOM FORMS

The comparison between ancient Near Eastern and biblical proverbs extends beyond content to form. Proverbs usually have a poetic punch to them; they say a lot in a few words. And biblical poetry, we have seen, has short, pithy lines heavy with imagery and grouped in parallelisms. Most of the early Egyptian instructions have extended poetic discourses similar

to that of Proverbs 1—9. Later instructions, like *Ankhsheshonqy*, are closer to the lists of sayings that we find in the second part of Proverbs. One
of the specific forms found in biblical and non-biblical works is the numerical proverb. Compare Proverbs 6:16-19 with a passage from a Ugaritic myth and from the *Ahiqar* text:

> *There are six things the LORD hates—*
>   *no, seven things he detests:*
> *Haughty eyes,*
>   *a lying tongue,*
>   *hands that kill the innocent,*
>   *a heart that plots evil,*
>   *feet that race to do wrong,*
>   *a false witness who pours out lies,*
>   *a person who sows discord in a family.*

> *Truly (there are) two sacrifices Baal hates, three the rider on the clouds—a sac-*
> *rifice of shame and a sacrifice of meanness and a sacrifice where handmaids de-*
> *bauch. (KTU 1.4. III. 17-21).*

> *There are two things which are good, and a third which is pleasing to Shamash:*
> *one who drinks and shares it, one who masters wisdom [and observes it]; and*
> *one who hears a word but tells it not. (lines 92-93a)[25]*

CONCLUSION

Our extensive survey of the similarities between ancient Near Eastern literature and the biblical book of Proverbs offers two powerful lessons, one
about how we view ancient times, and the other about how we view our
own times.

Perhaps the most important aspect of this kind of study is to help us
remember that Proverbs was not written yesterday. Proverbs is an ancient
book, firmly rooted in the ancient world. Modern translations obscure
this fact as they bring Proverbs up to date. The translators have gone back
into the ancient world so they can render the Hebrew text in a living, understandable, contemporary idiom, but many of the images and concepts
are still ancient. For that reason, Proverbs is not a book that should be

read just on the surface. Before we apply it to our lives, we must slow down, reflect, reconstruct its ancient setting, then use our intellect and imagination to make it relevant for the present.

This effort is also a healthy reminder that God spoke to his people in a language and a form that were current to their time—we have the job of making them current to our own.

This study of the similarities between the advice given in the biblical book and ancient Near Eastern wisdom also makes concrete what we read in 1 Kings 4, that the sages of Israel lived and studied in an international context. It is always dicey to be dogmatic about specific borrowings, but there is little doubt that Israel's wise teachers read, understood, adapted, and appropriated the wisdom of their (pagan!) neighbors.

Does this tell us something about how we should view our own, non-Christian culture, as well as other cultures worldwide? Many Christians react strongly against today's culture and the literature it produces—reading only Christian literature, going only to Christian schools, avoiding movies, and so forth. Certainly the prophets of Israel issued important warnings about the seductive power of pagan culture. The sages, though, are the counterbalance. They are a model of thoughtful observers, reflecting on the world around them. Perhaps we should be better observers ourselves.

Though the sages observed and appropriated, they never simply or uncritically borrowed ideas from the broader cultural setting. Rather they adapted them to their own religious values. Nowhere in Proverbs do we read about *Ma'at* or other pagan deities. If the sages observed a truth in Egyptian wisdom, they understood it to be a truth of Yahweh. They were in love with Woman Wisdom, and thus ultimately with Yahweh. Wisdom in Israel, in contrast to wisdom in the broader ancient Near East, is ultimately a relational concept. One enters into a relationship with wisdom, personified as a Woman; one is wise in proportion to the intimacy of that relationship:

> *Wisdom is a tree of life to those who embrace her;*
> *happy are those who hold her tightly. (Prov 3:18)*

FOR FURTHER REFLECTION

1. Are you convinced that there are true parallels between Proverbs and the literature of the ancient Near East? Does that bother you? encourage you? not interest you? fascinate you? Why or why not?
2. In what ways does knowing the broader ancient Near Eastern background of this biblical book help you understand it?
3. Why do you think God uses well-known and well-used literary genres to communicate his message to people?
4. Do you think the fact that God utilized the cultural and literary forms of the surrounding nations has any bearing on your witness in the world?

FOR FURTHER READING

Day, John, et al. Editors. *Wisdom in Ancient Israel.* Cambridge: Cambridge University Press, 1995.

Emerton, John A. "The Teaching of Amenemope and Proverbs XXII 17-XXIV 22: Further Reflections on a Long-Standing Problem." *Vetus Testamentum* 51 (2001): 431-57.

Gammie, John G., and Leo G. Perdue. *The Sage in Israel and the Ancient Near East.* Winona Lake, Ind.: Eisenbrauns, 1990.

Kitchen, Kenneth A. "Proverbs and Wisdom Books of the Ancient Near East." *Tyndale Bulletin* 28 (1977): 69-114.

Ruffle, J. "The Teaching of Amenemope and Its Connection with the Book of Proverbs." *Tyndale Bulletin* 28 (1977): 29-68.

Shupak, Nili. *Where Can Wisdom Be Found?: The Sage's Language in the Bible and in Ancient Egyptian Literature.* Göttingen: Vandenhoeck & Ruprecht, 1993.

Waltke, Bruce K. "The Book of Proverbs and Ancient Wisdom Literature." *Bibliotheca Sacra* 136 (1979): 302-17.

SEVEN

PROVERBS IN CONVERSATION
WITH JOB AND ECCLESIASTES

W hat would Job and the Teacher in Ecclesiastes say to "Solomon" about what Proverbs has to say concerning health and wealth and suffering? In a sense, this conversation goes on in Scripture, and we need to tune our ears to hear it.

Concerning health, the dominant note of Proverbs is optimistic:

> *Don't be impressed with your own wisdom.*
> *Instead, fear the LORD and turn away from evil.*
> *Then you will have healing for your body*
> *and strength for your bones. (Prov 3:7-8)*

The same primarily positive attitude characterizes book's attitude toward wealth and suffering:

> *I love all who love me.*
> *Those who search will surely find me.*
> *I have riches and honor,*
> *as well as wealth and justice.*
> *My gifts are better than gold, even the purest gold,*
> *my wages are better than sterling silver!*

I walk in righteousness,
  in paths of justice.
Those who love me inherit wealth.
  I will fill their treasuries. (Prov 8:17-21)

Granted that even the righteous don't escape the vicissitudes of life
completely, the message of Proverbs is that such troubles will be short-
lived:

The fears of the wicked will be fulfilled;
  so will the hopes of the godly.
When the storms of life come, the wicked are whirled away,
  but the godly have a lasting foundation. (Prov 10:24-25)

An initial reading of Proverbs might lead one to the conclusion that
those who follow the precepts of wisdom will be rewarded with great success, while those who embrace foolishness will encounter one obstacle after another. Indeed, that is the message Job's three "friends" and the
young Elihu seem to have heard and accepted from the book of Proverbs—at least at first glance.

THE WISDOM OF JOB'S THREE FRIENDS

If wisdom is basically the ability to navigate life's problems, then Job
needs a lot of wisdom. After all, he has a large problem. The prologue to
the book (Job 1—2) informs us that this previously prosperous and happy man has experienced one torment after another. Foreign raiders and
natural forces have devastated his property and killed his children. Finally, Job himself is covered with boils. In sudden succession, Job lost his
health and wealth and was plunged into unimaginable suffering.

Think of Job reading the passages from Proverbs quoted above. What
questions do you think he might have? To get some perspective on this
inquiry, we will examine Job's reaction to the three friends who had trav-
eled "to comfort and console him" (Job 2:11).

If Eliphaz, Bildad and Zophar really came with the intention of comfort, that soon changed after they heard Job's stinging lament (Job 3). In
response, they broke their silence and began a barrage of verbal attacks

on Job's attitude and thinking. This interchange between Job and his friends occupies a large portion of the book (Job 3—31). Indeed, there are three long cycles of dialogues between Job and Eliphaz, Bildad, and Zophar, as each of them speaks to Job and he responds to their arguments and accusations.

Though they address Job individually, close reading shows they are hammering away at Job with a common theme. The three friends represent the age-old wisdom of retribution theology. As we examine it, note that their thinking could be supported by proof texts from the book of Proverbs such as the verses we have already cited. However, as the friends apply this viewpoint to Job's situation, it becomes quite rigid and mechanical.

They start with the supposition that good things happen to good people and bad things happen to bad people. To put it in theological language, the righteous prosper and sinners suffer. Eliphaz, Bildad and Zophar go even further as they turn the equation of sin and suffering around. They insist that if you suffer, then you are a sinner. Job suffers, therefore he has sinned. If sin is Job's problem, there is only one solution to his difficulties: repentance. As wise men trying to give counsel to a friend in dire straits, they have the diagnosis (sin) as well as the remedy (repentance).

We see this, for instance, in Eliphaz's perspective as expressed in his first speech:

> *Stop and think!*
>   *When have the upright been destroyed?*
> *My experience shows that those who plant trouble*
>   *and cultivate evil will harvest the same.*
> *A breath from God destroys them.*
>   *They vanish in a blast of his anger.*
> *The lion roars and the wildcat snarls,*
>   *but the teeth of strong lions will be broken.*
> *The fierce lion will starve for lack of prey,*
>   *and the cubs of the lioness will be scattered. (Job 4:7-11)*

Job reacts strongly against this line of reasoning. He is suffering, but not because of his sin. Job nowhere argues that he is totally without sin;

he agrees with Bildad that no one can be righteous before God (Job 9:2). But he questions whether he can get justice from God. He directly counters the wisdom of his friends in 9:21-24:

I am innocent,
  but it makes no difference to me—
I despise my life.
Innocent or wicked, it is all the same to God.
  That's why I say, "He destroys both the blameless and the wicked."
When a plague sweeps through,
  he laughs at the death of the innocent.
The whole earth is in the hands of the wicked,
  and God blinds the eyes of the judges.
If he's not the one who does it, who is?

At the heart of the debate between Job and his friends is the question, Who is wise? Who has the correct insight into Job's suffering? Both Job and the friends set themselves up as sources of wisdom, and ridicule the wisdom of the other.

Zophar insults Job in 11:12:

An empty-headed person won't become wise
  any more than a wild donkey can bear a human child.

Job spares no punches in his counterattack and the assertion of his own wisdom:

You people really know everything, don't you?
  And when you die, wisdom will die with you!
Well, I know a few things myself—
  and you're no better than I am.
Who doesn't know these things you've been saying? (Job 12:2-3)

Your platitudes are as valuable as ashes.
  Your defense is as fragile as a clay pot. (Job 13:12)

We can feel the angry tension between Job and his friends. They are each vying for the solution to Job's problem of suffering. They are trying to navigate his difficulties, to get him on the right path again, the path to life. Job does not accept the friends' advice because, in essence, he does not regard them as his wisdom teachers. Instead, he offers his own interpretation—God is unfair (Job 9:21-24)—and his own solution—an interview with God to set God straight.

ELIHU'S WISDOM

The three friends run out of steam in their arguments against Job. They do not concede their point, but they make no headway either, and so they grow silent. Into this silence Elihu abruptly steps. At this point he has not been introduced. Indeed, as readers we have had no indication that there was anyone listening in on the previous debate.

Whereas Eliphaz, Bildad and Zophar represent the wisdom of the elders of the time, Elihu is a brash young man who thinks he has all the answers. He has waited patiently, so he says, out of respect for age, expecting the three friends to resolve the issue with Job. But they have failed, and he can remain silent no longer:

I am young and you are old,
*   so I held back from telling you what I think.*
I thought, "Those who are older should speak,
*   for wisdom comes with age."*
But there is a spirit within people,
*   the breath of the Almighty within them,*
*   that makes them intelligent.*
Sometimes the elders are not wise.
*   Sometimes the aged do not understand justice. (Job 32:6-9)*

Elihu cannot stand to see Job complacent in his pride: "Elihu . . . was angry because Job refused to admit that he had sinned and that God was right in punishing him" (Job 32:2). He is also deeply disappointed with the three friends: "He was also angry with Job's three friends, for they made God appear to be wrong by their inability to answer Job's arguments" (Job 32:3). So he sets himself up as still another wise man.

Mark this well, Job. Listen to me,
*   for I have more to say.*

But if you have anything to say, go ahead.
   Speak, for I am anxious to see you justified.
But if not, then listen to me.
   Keep silent and I will teach you wisdom. (Job 33:31-33)

What is striking in Elihu's speech, though, is that in spite of his claim
that he has something new to say (Job 32:14), he comes back to the same
old theology of retribution articulated by the three friends: Job suffers because he has sinned. Thus Elihu proclaims:

He [God] repays people according to their deeds.
   He treats people as they deserve.

He knows what they do,
   and in the night he overturns and destroys them.
He strikes them down because they are wicked,
   doing it openly for all to see.
For they turned away from following him.
   They have no respect for any of his ways.

For you have added rebellion to your sin;
   you show no respect,
   and you speak many angry words against God. (Job 34:11, 25-27, 37)

YAHWEH'S WISDOM

It is in Yahweh's speeches that we encounter the perspective on wisdom
that the book of Job wishes to impart to its readers.

Throughout the dialogues, Job urgently hopes for an interview with God:

My complaint today is still a bitter one,
   and I try hard not to groan aloud.
If only I knew where to find God,
   I would go to his court.
I would lay out my case
   and present my arguments.
Then I would listen to his reply
   and understand what he says to me.
Would he use his great power to argue with me?

No, he would give me a fair hearing.
Honest people can reason with him,
* so I would be acquitted once and for all by my judge.* *(Job 23:1-7)*

Job finally gets his wish as God appears to him in the form of a storm—an indication that he is coming in judgment (Ps 18; 29; Nahum 1). Job should have been careful what he wished for! The divine interview does not happen. Significantly, God never directly answers the question of why Job is suffering, except to rebuke him for casting aspersions on the divine reputation: "Will you discredit my justice and condemn me just to prove you are right?" (Job 40:8). Instead of directly justifying himself, God answers another question, that of the source of wisdom. This issue has been smoldering under the surface throughout the book. Now God provides the definitive answer: He alone is wise.

His first words from the storm set Job's wisdom in its place and introduce the next few chapters as God asks Job a series of questions that only the Creator could possibly answer:

Who is this that questions my wisdom
* with such ignorant words?*
Brace yourself like a man,
* because I have some questions for you,*
* and you must answer them.* *(Job 38:2-3)*

The questions that follow demonstrate God's full knowledge and control of the natural order that he created. Contrasted with this is Job's ignorance. The implication is that what is true of the natural order is also true for the moral order. God knows why Job suffered, but Job remains unanswered.

This conclusion to the matter of the source of wisdom is punctuated by a series of rhetorical questions that run through the divine speeches and ask about the source of wisdom more explicitly. Job 38:36-37 is illustrative (see also 39:13-18):

Who gives intuition to the heart
* and instinct to the mind?*
Who is wise enough to count all the clouds?

Job recognizes the power of God's speech and responds humbly and repentantly. He submits himself to the Almighty God of the universe and his will.

The conclusion of the book reverts to prose for the first time since the prologue. Now that Job has submitted to God, the three friends are rebuked, and the impetuous Elihu is ignored, God restores Job to his former glory and more. The ending promotes an attitude that acknowledges the power and wisdom of the God of the universe. This story truly ends on a happy note.

JOB'S MESSAGE ABOUT SUFFERING AND WISDOM

Job is a rich and complex book. I do not want to suggest that its message can be boiled down to a couple of pages of comment. Nonetheless, our concern is to examine how the book of Job helps us read Proverbs properly. I believe we can capture this under two headings: wisdom and suffering.

Wisdom. As we survey the plot and characters of the book of Job, the question of wisdom surfaces as the most important issue. Though the problem of suffering, specifically the suffering of the innocent, propels the story and is theologically important, the question "Who is wise?" takes precedence in the unfolding of the story line. Virtually all the characters of the book claim wisdom, but only at the end when God speaks out of the whirlwind is the issue settled. There is no contest; no human has a legitimate claim. God alone is the source of wisdom, and he contributes wisdom as he sees fit.

The proper human response, then, is repentance and submission. As Job himself says:

> *I had only heard about you before,*
> *but now I have seen you with my own eyes.*
> *I take back everything I said,*
> *and I sit in dust and ashes to show my repentance.* (Job 42:5-6)

Human suffering. God answers Job's question "Why do I suffer?" indirectly by answering the even more important question of wisdom. After all, no one escapes the pain of life. We are all anxious for an insight into the reason for our plight and perhaps some easing of the anguish.

While God chooses not to reveal the answer to this question to his human creatures, we still learn much about suffering from this book. For instance, if we do not learn why we suffer, the book does disabuse one common belief, the so-called doctrine of retribution.

The basic premise of retribution as represented by Eliphaz, Bildad and Zophar is, if you sin, then you will suffer. We have seen above that there is some truth to this premise. After all, Proverbs teaches that those who follow God's way, the way of wisdom, will "live in safety and be at ease, without fear of harm" (Prov 1:33).

The three friends, however, went far beyond the generally true proposition that sin leads to suffering. To reach the belief that anyone who suffers must have sinned, they reversed the cause and the effect. By doing that, they were saying that all suffering is explained by sin, that suffering is a telltale sign of sin. Job suffers; therefore, he has sinned. In the words of Proverbs, Job is not a wise man; he does not display the requisite righteous character.

But that is the importance of the book of Job, particularly in relation to the book of Proverbs. Job is a canonical corrective to this type of faulty reasoning. It guards against an overreading of the covenant and of the book of Proverbs. It denies a mechanical application of the connection in Proverbs between wise behavior and material reward. It does this by showing us a man whose suffering is for a reason other than his sin.

The reader has known since the prologue that Job's suffering is not caused by sin. Rather, he suffers for the same reason as the man we encounter in John 9, who was born blind. There the disciples' question reflects the same kind of retribution doctrine found on the lips of Job's three friends: "Rabbi, who sinned, this man or his parents, that he was born blind?" Jesus' response could also be applied to Job: "Neither this man nor his parents sinned, but this happened so that the work of God might be displayed in his life" (NIV). The difficult truth of Job and John 9—10 is that God is glorified through the suffering of his faithful servants.

The book of Job does not begin to explain all the reasons for suffering in the world. It rejects the retribution theory of the three friends as the only explanation of the origin of suffering. Job establishes once and for all that personal sin is not the only reason for suffering in this world.

ECCLESIASTES AND THE LIMITS OF PROVERBIAL WISDOM

Ecclesiastes is the third Old Testament wisdom book. Like Job, it serves as a check against an overly optimistic view of rewards promised to the wise based on the book of Proverbs. Ecclesiastes is an enigmatic and often controversial book;[1] here we will focus our brief comments on it as a canonical dialogue partner with Proverbs.

The main speaker in the book goes by the name "the Teacher" (see Eccles 1:12—12:8). According to the testimony of the unnamed author of the epilogue, the Teacher was a wise man (Eccles 12:9). As such, he apparently expected to live a prosperous and meaningful life. However, if one knows anything about the book of Ecclesiastes, it is that the Teacher comes to the distressing and shocking conclusion that life is "completely meaningless" (Eccles 1:2; 2:1, 15, 19; 3:19; 5:10; 6:11; 7:6; 8:10, 14; 9:9; 11:8; 12:8).

If we follow the Teacher's reasoning closely, we see that he reaches this conclusion in large part by realizing that the principle of retribution doesn't work in reality ("under the sun").

There are righteous people who are treated as if they did wicked deeds, and there are wicked people who are treated as if they did righteous deeds. (Eccles 8:14)

Both I observed in my meaningless life: There is a righteous person perishing in his righteousness, and there is a wicked person living long in his evil. (Eccles 7:15)

The latter passage leads to the following rather startling advice:

Do not be too righteous and do not be overly wise. Why ruin yourself? Do not be too wicked and do not be a fool. Why die when it is not your time? It is good that you hold on to this and also do not release your hand from that. The one who fears God will follow both of them. (Eccles 7:16-18)

So wisdom did not live up to the Teacher's expectations. It neither gave him joy in this life nor did he hope that it would defeat death ("How will the wise person die? Like the fool!" [Eccles. 2:16]). Thus, the Teacher pronounced wisdom itself meaningless (Eccles 2:12-17). But the Teacher's conclusions are not the conclusions of the book. A second wise man is using the Teacher's words to warn his son (12:12) about the dangers of "under the sun" thinking. These dangers are real because apart from God: life is difficult and then you die. That is why the book ends with the admonition:

> *Fear God and keep his commandments, for this is the whole duty of humanity. For God will bring every deed into judgment, including every hidden thing, whether good or evil.* (Eccles 12:13-14)

LISTENING TO THE DIALOGUE

By bringing the wisdom of Proverbs into conversation with the wisdom of the book of Job and Ecclesiastes, we acknowledge that the Bible is, after all, an organic whole. Certainly there are individual books with their unique emphases and contributions, so we must first study a book like Proverbs on its own. But it is also part of a larger collection, namely the Bible. In essence then, Proverbs does not stand alone, it is a chapter of a book. In other words, it has a context that is larger than itself. If we were to read Proverbs and conclude that the godly wise always live blessed lives, we would be wrong. Job was indeed "innocent," but he suffered terribly. The Teacher was a wise man, but found his life difficult and filled with doubt.

The teaching of Job and Ecclesiastes compels us to go back and read Proverbs more closely. The dominant note of the book should not be allowed to overwhelm the recognition that even Proverbs acknowledges that life is not black and white. For instance, in a later chapter, we will observe that, while many proverbs associate lasting wealth with the wise, other proverbs implicitly acknowledge that when a choice must be made between wealth and wisdom, one is much better off with wisdom (Prov 16:16).

Bruce Waltke, along with Raymond Van Leeuwen, has written well on these "counter-proverbs."[2] Waltke reminds us that proverbs are not promises. Though true as general principles, they are not true in every situation. It is usually, but not always the case, that the lazy are not rich. It is much more likely, but not a certainty, that a man will not contract a sexually transmitted disease if he is celibate or stays faithful to one woman. But again, Proverbs is aware—and Ecclesiastes and Job drive this home—that there are exceptions to the rule. It is cruel, then, to use a person's suffering as a tool for diagnosing their spiritual and ethical life.

Waltke goes on to suggest that the rewards of Proverbs ultimately need to be understood as extending beyond life. There is something to be considered in the controversial idea that Proverbs has a robust presentation of the afterlife.[3] And in light of the fuller teaching of the New Testament about the ultimate fate of the righteous and the wicked, we as Christian readers cannot help but have a fuller and richer understanding of the reward of life and death that we encounter in the book of Proverbs.

FOR FURTHER REFLECTION

1. Summarize in your own words the main point of the book of Job as described in the above chapter. Does it agree with your reading of the book up to this point?
2. What is Job's view of wisdom in particular? How does it relate to Proverbs? Is what they are saying the same thing, contradictory, in tension, or complementary of each other? Why?
3. How does reading Job affect the way you understand Proverbs?
4. Which book, Proverbs or Job, do you feel most naturally akin to? That is, which book reflects your basic understanding of how the world works?
5. What is bothering the Teacher? Do these things bother you as well?
6. Go back and read Proverbs 15 in the light of the message of Ecclesiastes. Does it affect your reading?
7. How does Jesus, the innocent sufferer, compare and contrast with Job, the innocent sufferer?
8. How is Christ the answer to the Teacher's worries and concerns?

FOR FURTHER READING

Bartholomew, Craig. *Reading Ecclesiastes*. Rome: Pontifical Biblical Institute, 1998.

Longman, Tremper, III. *Ecclesiastes*. NICOT. Grand Rapids, Mich.: Eerdmans, 1997.

Waltke, Bruce. "Does Proverbs Promise Too Much?" *Andrew University Seminary Studies* 34 (1966): 319-36.

Van Leeuwen, Raymond. "Wealth and Poverty: System and Contradiction in Proverbs." *Hebrew Studies* 33 (1992): 25-36.

Zerafa, Peter P. *The Wisdom of God in the Book of Job*. Rome: Herder, 1978.

EIGHT

PROVERBIAL WISDOM IN ACTION: JOSEPH AND DANIEL

The Bible presents us with ancient object lessons in the wisdom of Proverbs—among them, the stories of Joseph and Daniel. In their own way, both have been seen as embodying wisdom principles. Indeed, scholars in recent years have debated whether Genesis 37—50 as well as Daniel 1—6 should be classified as wisdom literature.[1] Whether they are wisdom literature or not, these stories clearly illuminate important themes that we have studied in Proverbs. We will illustrate this by looking at one story from each book.

JOSEPH IN POTIPHAR'S HOUSE: GENESIS 39

The story of Joseph is well known to even the most casual Bible reader, so I will be brief in reviewing the circumstances that lead up to the action of Genesis 39.[2] Genesis 37 introduces the sons of Jacob—who were born of different mothers: Leah and Rachel, Jacob's two wives, and Bilhah and Zilpah, two concubines. Rachel was by far Jacob's favorite, so her only son at this point,[3] Joseph, is also favored. Indeed, Jacob shows his preference for Joseph through gifts and special treatment, with the result that the other brothers hate Joseph.

One day, as the brothers are shepherding their father's flocks away from home, they seize the opportunity to get rid of Joseph, and end up selling him to Ishmaelite/Midianite traders. The traders take him down to Egypt and sell him into the household of an important Egyptian official named Potiphar.

Thus begins a series of events in which, on the human level, Joseph is seemingly subject to neglect and abuse by the other characters of the story. But from the perspective of the narrative, God is maneuvering his servant into a position within the Egyptian hierarchy so he might later rescue the family of God from the ravages of a death-dealing famine. At the conclusion of the narrative, Joseph himself articulates this divine perspective on his life as he addresses his brothers after the death of Jacob: "As far as I am concerned, God turned into good what you meant for evil. He brought me to the high position I have today so I could save the lives of many people" (Gen 50:20). God took evil human acts and used them for his own redemptive purposes.

Genesis 39 is a good example of this divine drama. After Potiphar purchases Joseph, his household explodes with prosperity. God is with Joseph—a theme echoing throughout the chapter—so God's blessing comes to Potiphar's life. Potiphar responds by giving this capable young man increased responsibility and privileges.

But one day Joseph is alone in the house with Potiphar's wife and she tries to seduce him into sleeping with her. (Looking at the story through the prism of the book of Proverbs, this woman is the "strange woman" of Proverbs, writ large on a human level, the embodiment of Woman Folly.) Joseph doesn't even bat an eye, but quickly rejects her advances by reminding her of the trust that her husband has placed in him. More important, perhaps, he invokes God: "How could I ever do such a wicked thing? It would be a great sin against God" (Gen 39:9)

In this we are reminded of the teaching about the immoral woman that we encountered in chapter three and will revisit in chapter eleven. Joseph well illustrates a young man who has heard the lesson of Proverbs 6:20-29:

My son, obey your father's commands,
  and don't neglect your mother's instruction.

Keep their words always in your heart.
  Tie them around your neck.
When you walk, their counsel will lead you.
  When you sleep, they will protect you.
  When you wake up, they will advise you.
For their command is a lamp
  and their instruction a light;
their corrective discipline
  is the way to life.
It will keep you from the immoral woman,
  from the smooth tongue of a promiscuous woman.
Don't lust for her beauty.
  Don't let her coy glances seduce you.
For a prostitute will bring you to poverty,
  but sleeping with another's man's wife will cost you your life.
Can a man scoop a flame into his lap
  and his clothes not catch on fire?
Can he walk on hot coals
  and not blister his feet?
So it is with the man who sleeps with another man's wife.
  He who embraces her will not go unpunished.

But Joseph is punished for his obedience. Falsely accused by Potiphar's wife, he is thrown into jail by his master (from Proverbs one would expect just the opposite, that his obedience would lead to blessing, not curse). How is it that the one who models the instructions of the father to the son in Proverbs meets this fate? It is only the beginning of the story.

In prison, Joseph meets the pharaoh's chief baker and chief cupbearer, high-ranking officials in the Egyptian court. Through personal experience they find out that God has granted Joseph wisdom in the matter of dream interpretation. They both have dreams that are relevant to their future, and Joseph interprets the dreams: the chief cupbearer will soon be released; the baker will soon meet his death at the hands of an angry pharaoh.

His interpretation comes true, and as the two officials leave to meet their respective fates, he reminds them to plead his case with their master.

However, again against expectations, they promptly forget about him. That is, until the pharaoh has a dream himself, and no one can interpret it. At that point the chief cupbearer remembers Joseph, who is then brought into Pharaoh's presence and interprets the dream. The pharaoh is so impressed that he places Joseph in a high position within his government. Here he not only protects the survival of Egypt and manipulates the radical increase in the pharaoh's power, but more importantly he is able to feed his family when they arrive from their famine-ravaged home, be reunited with them, and thus keep alive the recipients of God's promise.

Certainly, the events of Joseph's life took place long before the book of Proverbs was written. According to traditional dating of both books, the writing of Genesis also preceded that of Proverbs. Even so, we today cannot help but reflect on the event recorded in Genesis 39 in the light of Proverbs' teaching on the strange woman.

Thus we see, in this Old Testament context, an understanding that the connection between obedience and reward is not mechanical and definitely not immediate. In the long run Joseph's obedience leads to incredible blessing, but in the short run it leads to prison. Nonetheless, the path of wisdom is the only right path.

DANIEL VERSUS THE BABYLONIAN WISE MEN

The book of Daniel is known today primarily for its wild visions of the future found in the second half of the book. While the stories of Daniel 1–6 make up children's Sunday school curriculum, adult believers focus on trying to sort out the intricacies of the ancient prophecies. This is unfortunate for two reasons. The prophecies are not to be the stuff of titillating interpretive speculations, [4] and there is much of interest in the first six chapters. We will pause briefly at chapter 1, then proceed to a more substantial discussion of chapter 2.

In chapter 1, the biblical narrator reports that Nebuchadnezzar exerted pressure on Jerusalem, demanding that the people of Judah comply with his demands for submission. Recognizing that they were in no position to resist, the people agreed to Babylon's demands in two areas. They gave Nebuchadnezzar materials from the temple to take back to Babylon, and they turned over some of their young nobles who would return with him and be re-educated in Babylonian ways. In the ancient Near Eastern world, these were typical demands made by a dominant culture on a subordinate one.

Among the young nobles taken back to Babylon were Daniel and his three friends. This situation, of course, was potentially dangerous for these men. They would be expected to give in to Nebuchadnezzar's demands and become Babylonian in their outlook and loyalty. After their training, they would be put in service of the empire.

We learn quickly that Daniel and his friends are determined to retain their fidelity to their God. But can they survive in this hostile culture? In Daniel 1, we read the book's first account of how, in spite of present circumstances, God is in control and his people will survive and even thrive in exile.

But this did not come easily. There were many obstacles, the first of which was the king's insistence that the young men eat the rich food from his table. They refused, requesting only vegetables and water. The reason for this is not as evident as it may seem. Usual explanations—keeping kosher, refusing food offered to idols, rejection of political allegiance—are not consistent with the text as a whole.[5] Close analysis leads us to see that they did not want their later healthy appearance to be credited to the royal food, but to God who made them robust in spite of their meager diet.[6]

What reveals Daniel as a wise man in the proverbial sense is his ability to navigate life in spite of obstacles and regulate his emotions. Daniel's desire to avoid eating the rich food was stymied when the palace master refused to allow him and his friends the plain food they'd requested. At that point, Daniel did not exhibit anger, fear or disappointment; he did not throw a tantrum or slip into a depression. Rather, he considered the time and the circumstance, and found another way to reach his goal. At this point in the narrative, one thinks of the teachings in Proverbs about the calm-headed person and the impetuous person, and about thinking before acting:

> *People with understanding control their anger;*
> *a hot temper shows great foolishness. (Prov 14:29)*

> *Short-tempered people do foolish things,*
> *and schemers[7] are hated. (Prov 14:17)*

> *The wise are cautious and avoid danger;*
> *fools plunge ahead with reckless confidence. (Prov 14:16)*

Daniel knew that with patience he could gain his desired end and even stay in the good graces of the powers that be. This same wisdom characterized the advice that Proverbs gives:

> *The anger of the king is a deadly threat;*
> *the wise will try to appease it. (Prov 16:14)*

> *Whoever loves a pure heart and gracious speech*
> *will have the king as a friend. (Prov 22:11)*

> *Patience can persuade a prince,*
> *and soft speech can break bones. (Prov 25:15)*

Daniel's solution was to talk privately with the servant who delivered the king's rich food, asking that he bring only vegetables and water and after ten days assess the young men's appearance. If they looked sallow or weak, they would go back to the king's diet. This strategy is wise for a host of reasons, including the fact that the servant would have to dispose of the rich food—perhaps by "hiding it" in his stomach. It also allows him an out that assures him he will not be discovered.

The servant agreed, and Daniel and his friends took nothing but vegetables and water. After ten days, the four of them looked healthier than those eating the rich food. Eventually, Daniel and his friends so impressed the king that he assigned them to his court. And all the while, Daniel had the reassurance that his robust physical appearance was due not to the king's largesse but to God's supernatural intervention. Daniel's wisdom maneuvered through the obstacles and achieved a successful conclusion.

While the first chapter introduces Daniel as a wise man, the second chapter tells a story that exposes the depth of that wisdom. The episode begins with Nebuchadnezzar's dream, a dream that greatly disturbed his sleep. As might be anticipated in that culture, the king calls for his "magicians, enchanters, sorcerers and astrologers" (Dan 2:2)—a group later referred to as the "wise men" of Babylon (Dan 2:12). Daniel and his three friends were included in that group, having been trained in the language and literature of ancient Babylon, but they were not present when the king requested an interpretation.

So far everything was proceeding according to the expectations of the culture, but then the king threw a curve ball to the assembled group. He asked them not only to interpret the dream but to begin by telling him its contents. This was unheard of in the wisdom lore of ancient Babylon. Typically, the dreamer would describe the dream to the interpreters, then they would use reference works to determine its significance.[8] But Nebuchadnezzar refused to reveal the substance of the dream, so interpretation was impossible. This unprecedented situation led the wise men themselves to exclaim:

> *"There is not a man on earth who can do what the king asks! No king, however great and mighty, has ever asked such a thing of any magician or enchanter or astrologer. What the king asks is too difficult. No one can reveal it to the king except the gods, and they do not live among men." (Dan 2:10-11)*

The narrative is not crystal clear about why Nebuchadnezzar did this. Perhaps he had only a vague remembrance of the dream and needed the wise men to recreate the content. More likely, he was testing them. After all, making something up and passing it off as an authentic interpretation was all too easy. To actually describe the contents of another person's dream—that indeed would show a connection with the divine realm.

When the wise men could not comply, Nebuchadnezzar grew angry and decreed the death penalty for all Babylonian wise men, including Daniel and the three friends. When the king's messenger of death, Arioch, arrived at their house, Daniel did not panic. Instead, he asked for time. He then went to the other three and they turned to prayer. In response to the prayer, God revealed to the four the contents of the mysterious dream as well as its interpretation. Daniel informed Arioch, who quickly transported him to Nebuchadnezzar. Daniel then told the king about the dream of the multi-metalled statue and its connection to the future.[9]

This episode shows the qualitative difference between the ineffective wisdom of the Babylonian wise men and that of Daniel. The former were dependent on reference works and tradition, which were no help in telling the king the content of his dream. Daniel's wisdom, on the other hand, derived from God's revelation. After receiving the answer to his inquiry from God, Daniel praised God with language reminiscent of Proverbs 1:2-7:

> *Praise be to the name of God for ever and ever;*
> *wisdom and power are his.*
> *He changes times and seasons;*
> *he sets up kings and deposes them.*
> *He gives wisdom to the wise*
> *and knowledge to the discerning.*
> *He reveals deep and hidden things;*
> *he knows what lies in darkness,*
> *and light dwells with him.*
> *I thank and praise you, O God of my fathers:*
> *You have given me wisdom and power,*
> *you have made known to me what we asked of you,*
> *you have made known to us the dream of the king.* (Dan 2:20-23 NIV)

God, then, is the God of wisdom, and so he saves his faithful servants by revealing to them his knowledge. The theme of this chapter is that only God's wisdom can reveal the mysteries of life. So when Daniel stood before the king, he did not take credit for himself but rather proclaimed:

> *"No wise man, enchanter, magician, or diviner can explain to the king the mystery he has asked about, but there is a God in heaven who reveals mysteries. He has shown King Nebuchadnezzar what will happen in days to come."* (Dan 2:27-28 NIV)

FOR FURTHER REFLECTION

1. Do you agree that Joseph and Daniel are good examples of the wisdom teachings in the book of Proverbs?
2. Read Proverbs 14:19; 16:1,9; and especially 16:33. Then read the book of Esther in the light of these texts in Proverbs. Any connection?

3. Choose any chapter in Proverbs; with each proverb, ask if it is illustrated by a story elsewhere in the Old Testament.

FOR FURTHER READING

Longman, Tremper, III. *Daniel*. NIVAC. Grand Rapids, Mich.: Zondervan, 1998.

Rad, Gerhard von. "The Joseph Narrative and Ancient Wisdom." In *The Problem of the Hexateuch and Other Essays*. Edinburgh: Oliver & Boyd, 1966.

NINE

WHERE IS GOD IN PROVERBS?

Christ, the Treasure of God's Wisdom

The relationship between the Old and New Testaments is an important yet debated question. Intelligent and informed interpreters take different positions on exactly how the two testaments are related. Some people think it quite wrong to read the Old Testament in the light of the New. After all, the New Testament was written centuries after the most recent books of the Old. To read the message of the New Testament back into that ancient text can lead to distortions and an obscuring of the particular witness of the Old Testament priests, prophets, and wisdom teachers. Other people never read the Old Testament on its own, but only through the prism of the New Testament.

What is true of the Old Testament as a whole is true also of the book of Proverbs. Readers may, for instance, never consider the ancient setting of the book but rather read it as if it were written yesterday. Others carefully keep its message separate from that of the New Testament.

As is usual in such debates, the truth is found between the extremes. In order to preserve the integrity of the message, it is important to first interpret the book in its ancient, original setting, to ask how the original audience understood its words. For example, they would understand the choice between Woman Wisdom and Woman Folly to be, in fact, a life-

or-death choice between Yahweh, the true God, and idols, particularly Baal and Asherah.

Once this is established, though, it is hard to understand why Christian readers would not go further and read the book again in the light of the New Testament. Jesus himself insists on such a reading of the Old Testament in two postresurrection appearances recorded in Luke 24. In the first, he joins two disciples on the road to Emmaus and learns how distraught they are over the collapse of their hope at the death of Jesus. Though they do not recognize him, he addresses their distress:

> *"You are such foolish people. You find it so hard to believe all that the prophets wrote in the Scriptures. Wasn't it clearly predicted by the prophets that the Messiah would have to suffer all these things before entering his time of glory?" Then Jesus quoted passages from the writings of Moses and all the prophets, explaining what all the Scriptures said about himself. (Lk 24:25-27)*

And again, a little later in the Gospel, he responds to a broader group of disciples:

> *"When I was with you before, I told you that everything written about me by Moses and the prophets and in the Psalms must all come true." Then he opened their minds to understand these many Scriptures. (Lk 24:44-45)*

In essence, Jesus is disclosing that the entirety of the Old Testament anticipated his coming suffering and glorification.

To view this from another perspective, it was the coming of Jesus that revealed a deeper meaning within the holy writings of Israel. It is not that it was a previously hidden meaning or that it involves the imposition of a foreign code on the words. No, the Messiah of Israel was expected well before he came. But his coming clarified the earlier revelation.

A rough, though imperfect analogy may be found in a good murder mystery. The first part of the book makes sense on its own terms, but as the ending comes closer and the plot is brought to resolution, the first part of the book takes on a newer, deeper meaning. Hints or clues unnoticed in the initial reading would be glaringly obvious in a subsequent reading.

I will hazard one further example from the popular 1999 movie *The Sixth Sense*. In this critically acclaimed work, Bruce Willis plays the lead character, a psychologist who is treating a young man being tormented by visions of the dead. Willis treats his patient with compassion, but he understands the visions to be hallucinatory. In the meantime, Willis is struggling with his own problems, including a growing distance between himself and his wife, ever since he was almost killed by an intruder. As it unfolds, the story makes perfect sense to the audience, but it takes on a new meaning with the revelation at the end that Willis himself is dead. He wasn't almost killed by the intruder; he was killed. His estrangement from his wife is not psychological; it is spiritual: She is alive and he is dead. This plot twist is a complete surprise, but once it comes, the audience cannot see the first part with the same understanding as they did previously. The success of the plot hinges, in large part, on its making sense with both "readings."

This analogy is limited because, as I mentioned earlier, the ancient audience of the Old Testament already anticipated the Messiah; but when Jesus came, the picture grew clearer. No one expected a suffering, crucified messiah—especially if we take seriously the report in the Gospels of reactions to Jesus' crucifixion. But once it happened, a whole host of Old Testament prophecies became clearer (Isaiah 53 among them).

This lengthy treatment of a central issue of interpretive theory, or hermeneutics, is important as we make our next move toward understanding how to read the book of Proverbs. Does Proverbs anticipate Christ? We begin with a closer look at Proverbs 8.

A CLOSER LOOK AT WOMAN WISDOM: PROVERBS 8

Wisdom describes her integral involvement with creation in Proverbs 8:22-31:

> *The LORD formed me* [qanani] *from the beginning* [re'sit],
> *before he created anything else.*
> *I was appointed* [nissakti] *in ages past,*
> *at the very first, before the earth began.*
> *I was born* [holalti] *before the oceans* [t°homot] *were created,*

before the springs bubbled forth their waters.
Before the mountains were formed,
 before the hills, I was born [holalti]—
before he had made the earth and fields
 and the first handfuls of soil.
I was there when he set the clouds above,
 when he established springs deep in the earth.
I was there when he set the limits of the seas,
 so they would not spread beyond their boundaries.
And when he marked off the earth's foundations,
 I was the architect ['amon] *at his side.*
I was his constant delight,
 rejoicing always in his presence.
And how happy I was with what he created—
 I rejoiced with all the human family!

This magnificent poem reflects on Wisdom's role at creation. As we
will have a number of occasions to point out, however, the largest interpretive error made when reading this poem is to lose sight of its literary
form. It is a highly figurative composition. It should not be read in a strict-
ly literal fashion. To do so makes no sense in its original context, and
when applied to its later use, it creates great theological damage (see
"Jesus Is God's Wisdom," below).

We have already observed that Woman Wisdom is a personification of
God's attribute of wisdom. This part of the poem is making the point that
God created the cosmos by virtue of his age-old wisdom. The language
about the creation of Wisdom is a powerful metaphor, affirming that
God's wisdom preceded every other thing. It is figurative language; Wisdom is not a separate personal entity. That it is provocative language is
not to be doubted and is confirmed by the fact that certain minor but ar-
ticulate strands of Judaism and Christianity came to treat Wisdom as a
separate divine being, even a bride of Yahweh himself (see below).

In defense against such moves, monotheistic interpreters have been
tempted to understand some of the poem's terminology in a different fashion than translated above. For instance, the verb *qanani,* here rendered

"formed me," has been understood by some interpreters as coming from a different root, one that sounds the same but means "acquired me." In my judgment that translation is heavy-handed and unnecessary; it forgets that we are interpreting a poem.

And a powerful poem it is. Notice all of the language that reminds us of Genesis 1. It begins "The LORD formed me from the beginning (*reshit*)," reminiscent of the very first verse of the Bible: "In the beginning (*bᵉreshit*) God created the heavens and the earth" (Gen 1:1). Later, when the poet says "I was born before the oceans were created," the word "oceans" (*tᵉhomot*) echoes the *tᵉhom* over which the Spirit of God hovered (Gen 1:2). The pushing back of the waters and the establishment of their boundaries (Prov 8:29) recall the pushing back of the waters to form the dry ground on the third day (Gen 1:9-13). The parallels go on and on, showing a close connection between Wisdom and creation.

Indeed, Wisdom was not only there, but was the agency through which creation came into existence. The NLT in my opinion correctly renders the rare Hebrew word *'amon* in 8:30 as "architect."[1] It was through divine Wisdom that the world came to be.

We will develop this thought further in another section, but one point needs noting now. To anyone who looks out at the world—whether the original audience of Proverbs or ourselves today—it does not appear, at least initially, to be created by wisdom. Rather, chaos impinges on order. At the most mundane level, there is trash to be taken out, laundry to be done, floors to be swept—without end. At the most profound level, there are tornadoes and earthquakes, poverty and alienation, and death. Yet Genesis 1, and its reflection in Proverbs 8:22-31, inform us that the world was not created chaotically. God, through his wisdom, created an order that he himself could rejoice in. Indeed, it was a two-way street since Wisdom rejoiced—or played— not only with God, but also with humanity:

> *I was his constant delight,*
> *rejoicing always in his presence.*
> *And how happy I was with what he created—*
> *I rejoiced with all the human family! (Prov 8:30-31)*

The connection between Wisdom and creation assures us that creation's order has not been completely eradicated. So, to live well, to live wisely, is to live in harmony with the creation—as the book of Proverbs teaches. Thus, we do well to study creation, recognizing the disruption of sin, in order to find the right way to navigate life.

JESUS IS GOD'S WISDOM

The Gospels. Even before Jesus begins his ministry, we see evidence of the Gospel writers' interest in him as a wise person. Of the two Gospels that report his birth and youth, Luke shows a special interest in Jesus' wisdom. For instance, after Jesus is born, we learn twice that this young man grew physically but also "with wisdom beyond his years" (Luke 2:40, cf. also 2:52 NLT). These two notices surround a story that gives us Christ's wisdom, and it too comments on one of the few events related to us from Jesus' youth.

Like good Jewish parents, Mary and Joseph took their son every year to Jerusalem for the Passover. When Jesus was twelve, they made the trip as usual, but this time, as they returned to Nazareth, they panicked when they realized that Jesus was not with them. With fear in their hearts, they rushed back to Jerusalem and spent three days frantically searching for him. They finally discovered him in the Temple "sitting among the religious teachers, discussing deep questions with them" (Luke 2:46 NLT). People were watching with amazement "at his understanding and his answers" (Luke 2:47 NLT). After all, he wasn't speaking with just anyone, he was in a discussion with the leading theologians of his day, and they were paying attention to what he was saying. Here is a child who reflects God's wisdom.

When Jesus began his ministry, people recognized him as a wise teacher. In Mark's first report of his teaching, we hear the people's reaction: "Jesus and his companions went to the town of Capernaum. When the Sabbath day came, he went into the synagogue and began to teach. The people were amazed at his teaching, for he taught with real authority—quite unlike the teachers of religious law" (Mk 1:21-22). Later, in Nazareth, those who knew him while he was growing up also acknowledge his gifts: "Where did he get all his wisdom and the power to perform such miracles?" (Mk 6:2).

The most characteristic form of Jesus' teaching, the parable, was part of the repertoire of the wisdom teacher. Indeed, the Hebrew word (*mashal*) was translated into the Greek word "parable" (*parabole*). Accordingly, it is no stretch to say that Jesus was a first-century wisdom teacher.

Jesus recognized himself as wise and condemned those who rejected his wisdom. In Luke 11:31, he tells the crowd: "The queen of Sheba will rise up against this generation on judgment day and condemn it, because she came from a distant land to hear the wisdom of Solomon. And now someone greater than Solomon is here—and you refuse to listen to him" (NLT).

The New Testament Epistles. While the Gospels demonstrate that Jesus was wise—indeed, wiser than Solomon—Paul asserts that Jesus is not simply wise; he is the very incarnation of God's wisdom. Twice Paul identifies Jesus with God's wisdom. First in 1 Corinthians, a passage that will occupy our attention later, he says, "God made Christ to be wisdom itself" (1 Cor 1:30). Second, in Colossians 2:3 Paul proclaims that in Christ "lie hidden all the treasures of wisdom and knowledge." With this as background, it is not surprising that the New Testament subtly associates Jesus with Woman Wisdom, particularly as presented in Proverbs 8.

Jesus and Woman Wisdom. In Matthew 11, Jesus addresses opponents who argued that John the Baptist was ascetic in his lifestyle, while Jesus was too celebratory. Notice the final assertion in his reply:

> For John came neither eating nor drinking, and they say, "He has a demon." The Son of Man came eating and drinking, and they say, "Here is a glutton and a drunkard, a friend of tax collectors and 'sinners.'" But wisdom is proved right by her actions. (Mt 11:18-19 NIV)

In that last sentence, Jesus claims that his behavior represents the behavior of Woman Wisdom herself.

Elsewhere in the New Testament Jesus is described in language that is reminiscent of Proverbs 8. We turn first to Colossians 1:15-17:

Christ is the visible image of the invisible God.
  He existed before anything was created and is supreme over all creation,
for through him God created everything on earth.
He made the things we can see
    and the things we can't see—
such as thrones, kingdoms,
    rulers, and authorities in the unseen world.
Everything was created through him and for him.
He existed before anything else,
    and he holds all creation together.

Though clearly not a quotation from Proverbs, this text would be recognized by someone well versed in the Old Testament, as Paul was, that Jesus occupies the place of Wisdom. Indeed, the literal rendition of the Greek of the sentence that ends "is supreme over all creation" is "He is the firstborn of all creation."[2] Paul is inviting a comparison: Wisdom was firstborn in Proverbs 8; Jesus is firstborn in Colossians. Wisdom is the agent of divine creation in Proverbs; Christ is the agent in Colossians. In Proverbs 8 we read:

Because of me, kings reign,
    and rulers make just decrees.
Rulers lead with my help,
    and nobles make righteous judgments (Prov 8:15-16)

And in Colossians 1:16, Christ made "kings, kingdoms, rulers, and authorities." The message is clear: Jesus is Wisdom herself.

The author of Revelation is a further witness to the connection between Wisdom and Jesus. In the introduction to the letter to the church at Laodicia, we read "This is the message from the one who is the Amen—the faithful and true witness, the ruler of God's new creation" (Rev 3:14). The last phrase (*hē arxē tēs ktiseōs tou theou*) resonates with the ideas behind Proverbs 8:22-30. In particular, the phrase may represent the meaning of that difficult word in Proverbs 8:30, the "architect" (*'ammon*) of creation. The allusion is subtle but clear: Jesus stands in the place of Woman Wisdom.

Even more subtly, we might note that the great preface to the Gospel of John resonates with language reminiscent of the poem about Woman Wisdom in Proverbs 8. The Word of God (the Logos), who is God himself (Jn 1:1), was "in the beginning with God. He created everything there is." Indeed, the "world was made through him." Jesus, of course, is the Word, and the association is with language reminiscent of Woman Wisdom.

WARNING: TREAT AS POETRY

Before pressing on with the significance of this association between Wisdom and Christ, I need to issue a warning. This warning is directed toward a basic misunderstanding of the relationship between Christ and Wisdom that has led to the most damaging theological consequences possible. In a word, we must remember the metaphorical quality of Proverbs 8 and its relationship with the New Testament passages.

Notice well that I don't say that Woman Wisdom is *just* a metaphor. That would imply that metaphor is a weak form of communication, and nothing could be more misguided. A metaphor is a powerful vehicle of meaning. It brings into comparison two things that are really not like each other except in a certain manner. By bringing together two fundamentally dissimilar things, a metaphor is supposed to shock the reader into paying attention and asking where the true connection is to be found.

The Lord is my father. Really? I have a wonderful father, whom I love dearly. I could fill this page with his accomplishments and the good side of his character. But the father I know has made mistakes; he's also had sextuple bypass surgery. He can be demanding and unreasonable. The Lord, then, is not to be identified with my father or any other human father. But the comparison is fruitful once we ask the question: In what way is the Lord like my father? In this case, I remember how my father provided for my needs, both physical and spiritual. How much he loved me and my mother and sisters. How he would have given his life for his family. Even those who have evil fathers still have a sense of what a good father is like, and that image helps them unpack the metaphor of God as their father.

Proverbs 8 associates the Lord with a woman named Wisdom. As we have seen, this metaphor teaches us many rich things about who God is and our relationship with him. But God is not Woman Wisdom. We may not use this metaphor to teach that the Lord is female any more than we may use the image of God as king, father or warrior to argue that God is male. We may not use Proverbs 8 to suggest, against the biblical teaching that God is one, that there is a separate deity created at the beginning of time.

We must remember all this when we see that Jesus associates himself with Wisdom in the New Testament. Woman Wisdom is not a pre-incarnate form of the second person of the Trinity. Jesus is not to be identified with Wisdom. The language about Jesus being the "firstborn of creation" is not to be pressed literally as if Jesus were a created being. But—and this is crucial—the association between Jesus and Woman Wisdom in the New Testament is a powerful way of saying that Jesus is the embodiment of God's Wisdom.

THE CHOICE REVISITED

Seeing Jesus as the embodiment of God's Wisdom has important implications for how Christians read Proverbs 1—9. Make no mistake, we must understand the choice between the two Women first on its ancient terms. It is a choice between Yahweh and the idols, particularly Baal. However, after reading the New Testament we cannot read the Old in exactly the same way. We have been introduced to Jesus as the Wisdom of God. To embrace Woman Wisdom is to enter a relationship with Jesus Christ.

The obverse is equally relevant. I know no one who has seriously claimed to be a follower of Baal in the twenty-first century. Is then Woman Folly no longer a threat to the worship of Yahweh? Of course she is still dangerous, but under different forms.

Idolatry, whether in ancient or modern times, consists of taking any bit of the creation and promoting it to the position of the creator (Rom 1:21-23). In the Old Testament, God's people often went astray by worshiping false gods. These false gods were empty, nothing, nonexistent—on one level. However, there are hints in the text that, on another level, these gods had power. After all, God defeated the Egyptian gods with the plagues (Ex 12:12), even though initially they had the ability to mimic some of the earlier, easier miracles, like turning a staff into a serpent (Ex 7:1-13).

As we turn to the New Testament, we get a clearer understanding not only of God but also of the dark forces of the universe. What then stands in the place of Woman Folly in our modern lives? Not Baal, but perhaps other things or people that we consider more important than Jesus: money, power, pleasure, addictions. Behind those idols stands a supernatural power, presented as a personal being, known as Satan or the devil. The choice that stands before us in Proverbs 9, embodied Women Wisdom and Women Folly, is, do we dine with Jesus or with the devil?

THE SHADOW OF WOMAN WISDOM

We began our exploration of Proverbs 1—9 with the question of the theology of the book as a whole. It is easy, we observed, to isolate certain proverbs from the second part of the book and treat them as human-centered advice based on experience. Such is the case in the following example:

A wise child brings joy to a father;
  a foolish child brings grief to a mother.
Tainted gain has no lasting value,
  but right living can save your life.
Lazy people are soon poor;
  hard workers get rich.
A wise youth harvests in the summer;
  but one who sleeps during harvest is a disgrace. (Prov 10:1-2, 4-5)

To be sure, there is an occasional mention of God, as in Proverbs 10:3, the verse I skipped in the quotation above:

The LORD will not let the godly go hungry,
  but he refuses to satisfy the craving of the wicked.

But most of the isolated, pithy sayings in Proverbs 10—31 seem to have no quality of special revelation and offer no comment on how they are connected with Yahweh. They just seem like accurate observations and sage advice on how to get along in the world. The only reason I quoted Proverbs 10:1-6 is because these are the first examples in the second part of the book; any other quotation from chapters 10-31 would evoke the same observation.

However, now that we have taken a close look at Proverbs 1—9, we can see how it is impossible to read any single proverb in the latter part of the book as purely secular. The entire book is drenched in theology. A proverbial observation becomes a thermometer of one's relationship with Woman Wisdom, who is Yahweh, and a command or admonition is a command or admonition that is implicitly from the Woman herself.

Take the first set of proverbs just quoted:

A wise child brings joy to a father;
   a foolish child brings grief to a mother.

This observation has an implicit directive built in. It does not give a command, but its effect is to lead us to ponder our relationship with a parent. We might reason in the following way. If I bring joy to my parents, then I am wise. That means my behavior reveals that I am in relationship with Woman Wisdom, which means that I am a follower of Yahweh. As a Christian, it shows that I am aligned with the one who is the treasure of God's wisdom, namely Christ. Or we might be forced to conclude: If I bring grief to my parents, then I demonstrate that I am in the arms of Woman Folly. Extended to the metaphorical world of the competing loves of Woman Wisdom and Woman Folly, if I am a foolish son, then I have the heart of an adulterer. With a New Testament reading, I am really in league with the devil.

FOR FURTHER REFLECTION

1. Describe in your own words the relationship between the Old and New Testaments that has been presented in this chapter. Do you agree or disagree?
2. How is Jesus related to Woman Wisdom?
3. What makes Jesus wise? How does Jesus make us wise?
4. Does the Old Testament's female imagery for God bother you? Why or why not?

5. Woman Folly stands for idols that tempt us to worship them. What are some tempting idols in your life?

FOR FURTHER READING

Longman, Tremper, III. *Reading the Bible with Heart and Mind.* Colorado Springs, Colo.: NavPress, 1997.

Witherington, Ben, III. *Jesus the Sage: The Pilgrimage of Wisdom.* Minneapolis: Fortress, 1994.

3

FOLLOWING THE THEMES
IN PROVERBS

■ ■ ■

TEN

HOW TO STUDY THEMES
IN PROVERBS

Money Matters

P roverbs bombards the reader with pithy advice about a host of subjects. Even if, as some believe, the book is organized at some deep level or through incidental catchwords, that does not seem to help the reader. Experienced readers of the book, as well as novices, can be overwhelmed by the diversity of topics and the apparent random order in which they are presented. As an anthology, or collection, Proverbs has numerous duplicate and near-duplicate sayings (i.e., Prov 19:5 and 19:9)—which indicates a long growth of the book from more than one source.[1] The final editors of the book were not interested in putting it into the kind of order that would appeal to modern Western logic.[2]

The ancient sage apparently would know the book so well that circumstances would call to mind the relevant proverb for application. For us, however, it is helpful to take a theme or topic addressed in the book, isolate the relevant proverbs, then study them as a group. Perhaps this is a concession to the thinking patterns of our day. We like things organized and systematically presented. As we study a topic, though, we should be careful not to make the book speak in too harmonious or logical a fashion. In other words, in keeping with the nature of the book as we have described it so far, we should not be surprised if we discover proverbs on the same subject that seem at odds with one another. As we have seen, the application of a proverb depends on the circumstance and the people involved.

Our topic is money, though the term may be an anachronism, depending on when the book of Proverbs was written (see appendix 1). Money in the form of coins did not develop until very late in the Old Testament time period. It was an innovation of the Persians, the empire that enveloped all the ancient Near East, including Palestine, from the latter half of the sixth century to 333 B.C. when Greek rule started under Alexander the Great. However, from the dawn of history, people have used goods, precious metals, flocks and herds, and other commodities as a means of exchange.

We begin with a brief overview of Proverbs' teaching on the subject of wealth and poverty.[3] Judged by the number of proverbs dedicated to this theme, it is certainly one of the most important in the book. Other large themes include proper relationships with women (remember that the book is addressed primarily to men), wise use of speech and wisdom itself.

The benefits of such a thematic study are at least twofold. First, it allows any reader to become involved with the entire text, interacting with it at a deeper level as well as learning important principles for navigating life. Second, it provides the basis for an interesting series of lessons or sermons on the various topics covered by Proverbs. In either case, however, we need to guard that such studies do not devolve into simply a number of moral or practical principles. To do so would be to read the text outside its theological context, a context that encompasses both the book and the whole of Scripture. As we have seen, reading in context is a fundamental principle in biblical interpretation.

THE PROCEDURE

In undertaking such a study, the first step is to read through the whole book, noting those verses that bear on the topic we are interested in—in our case, wealth and poverty. This may sound mechanical, but it isn't, at least not entirely. While certain passages are clearly relevant, others will require making a decision. For example, what about Proverbs 17:1?

> *Better a dry crust eaten in peace*
> *than a great feast with conflict.*

I ended up including it, since a great feast occurs only with the expenditure of considerable resources, whereas a dry crust can be obtained even by the poor. I found also that it fit in with other passages on poverty and wealth.

As I reviewed the book of Proverbs for its teaching on poverty and wealth, I found more relevant passages than I had anticipated. I made a list of the references so I could study them together, but also because I wanted to remain mindful of where they occurred so I could see if there was a broader context that might illuminate my understanding—sometimes proverbs are in pairs or larger groups. (For the purposes of this chapter, I chose just a few proverbs to represent the many-sided teaching of the book of Proverbs on money.)

My next step was to type out the relevant proverbs and read them together for a number of days. In trying to understand what each was saying about wealth and poverty, I began to see that they also fit into a few broad categories (which is how I will present them here). I also noted, as I sought to fit them together, that sometimes they seemed at odds with one another. For instance, some proverbs invite the thought that wealth comes only to hard-working, righteous, wise people, while others seem to say that evil people can be rich. For example:

> *The blessing of the LORD makes a person rich,*
> *and he adds no sorrow with it. (Prov 10:22)*

> *Better to be poor and honest*
> *than rich and crooked. (Prov 28:6)*

How do such apparently contradictory proverbs stand together? That is the type of question that needs to be answered at this step of our inquiry.

Finally, it is critical, when applying the book's wisdom to our lives, to go beyond the particular texts we have been studying to see how their teaching fits into the rest of the book of Proverbs, the Old Testament and the Bible as a whole. In particular, we would want to study the New Testament teaching on wealth and poverty, asking ourselves if the texts we are studying in Proverbs anticipate Jesus in some way.

PROVERBS ON WEALTH AND POVERTY

After studying the passages, I settled on the following seven categories of what Proverbs says about wealth and poverty:

- God blesses the righteous with wealth.
- Foolish behavior leads to poverty.
- The wealth of fools will not last.
- Poverty is the result of injustice and oppression.
- Those with money must be generous.
- Wisdom is better than wealth.
- Wealth has limited value.

God blesses the righteous with wealth. Proverbs has been criticized in modern days for siding with the wealthy and neglecting the poor. As we will soon see, this is much too simplistic a reading of the book's teaching. Nonetheless, it is true that the book of Proverbs asserts that God blesses his people with material gain. Indeed, the very first word the book gives us on wealth suggests that God rewards those who honor him:

> Honor the LORD with your wealth
>   and with the best part of everything you produce.
> Then he will fill your barns with grain,
>   and your vats with good wine. (Prov 3:9-10)

Observe the connection between right action and material reward. The setting of this saying is clearly agricultural, but the principle transfers easily to other areas. We do well, however, to remember that proverbs are snapshots of reality, generally true principles, but not promises. A statement such as Proverbs 3:9-10 is not a formula for success. Nonetheless, this proverb is making the claim that there is a relationship between spiritual values and one's wealth, and one might expect to gain materially if one honors the Lord with wealth.

Further on in the same discourse, we hear that wealth is a consequence of wisdom, here personified as a woman with gifts:

Wisdom is more precious than rubies;
  nothing you desire can compare with her.
She offers you long life in her right hand,
  and riches and honor in her left. (Prov 3:15-16)

How can Wisdom be more precious than rubies? Remember the young Solomon, who could ask God for anything, and pleases the Lord no end by requesting wisdom. The result: "I will do what you have asked. I will give you a wise and discerning heart, so that there will never have been anyone like you, nor will there ever be. Moreover, I will give you what you have not asked for—both riches and honor" (1 Kings 3:12-13). So, Wisdom can give rubies, and then some. In Proverbs as well as in Solomon's life, it has its material rewards. One of the most optimistic statements of this is Proverbs 10:22:

The blessing of the LORD makes a person rich,
  and he adds no sorrow to it.

What is the advantage of wealth to the wise? Proverbs provides an answer. It makes life's obstacles easier to navigate:

The wealth of the rich is their fortress;
  the poverty of the poor is their disaster. (Prov 10:15)

The first part of Proverbs 10:16 supports this idea when it states, "the earnings of the godly enhance their lives." But Proverbs 14:24 shows the flip side of this optimistic outlook:

Wealth is a crown for the wise;
  the effort of fools yields only foolishness.

So far, we have seen sufficient examples to show that Proverbs associates wisdom and wealth. But this is far from the end of the story. As we will see next, the wise are not the only ones with money.

Foolish behavior leads to poverty. If wisdom and its associated behaviors lead to riches, then we are not surprised to find that Proverbs teaches that the reverse is true as well: Folly results in poverty. This is especially clear in the contrast drawn between those who work hard and those who are lazy. In Proverbs, laziness is seen as the epitome of foolish behavior. Various proverbs poke fun at the lazy person:

The lazy person claims, "There might be a lion on the road!
   Yes, I'm sure there's a lion out there!"
As a door swings back and forth on its hinges,
   so the lazy person turns over in bed.
Lazy people take food in their hand
   but don't even lift it to their mouth. (Prov 26:13-15)

These proverbs use hyperbole to ridicule lazy people. The first accuses the lazy of making up lame excuses for not going out and getting to work. The second dwells on the propensity of sluggards to spend too much time in bed. The last creates the absurd picture of people who will not expend enough energy even to meet their basic needs.

Such foolish behavior leads to poverty, both in general and in the common endeavor of raising food:

Lazy people are soon poor;
   hard workers get rich. (Prov 10:4)

A wise youth harvests in the summer,
   but one who sleeps during harvest is a disgrace. (Prov 10:5)

The humorous and biting picture of the fool is meant to motivate those who are walking the wrong path. The extended discourse found in Proverbs 6:6-11 gives a pointed example:

Take a lesson from the ants, you lazybones.
   Learn their ways and become wise!
Though they have no prince
   or governor or ruler to make them work,
They labor all summer,
   gathering food for the winter.
But you, lazybones, how long will you sleep?
   When will you wake up?

A little extra sleep, a little more slumber,
  a little folding of the hands to rest—
then poverty will pounce on you like a bandit;
  scarcity will attack you liked an armed robber.

Though laziness is the most frequently cited reason for poverty, other reasons are given as well. One of these is over-indulgence, which Proverbs 21:17 describes:

Those who love pleasure become poor;
  wine and luxury are not the way to riches.

Another reason for poverty is oppression of the poor—especially by those who are already rich.

A person who gets ahead by oppressing the poor
  or by showering gifts on the rich will end in poverty. (Prov 22:16)

Does this mean that frugality is one avenue to wealth? Not according to Proverbs 11:24:

Give freely and become more wealthy;
  be stingy and lose everything.

To paraphrase the well-known poem in Ecclesiastes 3:1-8, there appears to be a time for giving and a time for saving. Those who ignore this, especially in their dealings with the poor and their use of luxuries, are likely to join the lazy as candidates for poverty.

The wealth of fools will not last. Experience teaches us that the first two snapshots are not always the case. There are rich fools and poor people who are wise. What's going on? That this question bothered the wise is seen in Psalm 73:

For I envied the proud
  when I saw them prosper despite their wickedness.
They seem to live such painless lives;
  their bodies are so healthy and strong.
They aren't troubled like other people
  or plagued with problems like everyone else.

They wear their pride like a jeweled necklace,
    and clothe themselves with cruelty. . . .
Look at these wicked people—
    enjoying a life of ease while their riches multiply. (Ps 73:3-6, 12)

Though the book of Proverbs does not struggle with this issue as intensely as do Ecclesiastes and Job, it does recognize that wealth is ephemeral and easily perverted. Its admonitions, though they might not say so expressly, are rooted in the awareness that foolish, even shady people, are wealthy, that lazy people can inherit money from hard-working parents, that acquiring and maintaining wealth is fraught with dangers, and that wealth is often superficial and temporary. So it can say:

Evil people get rich for the moment,
    but the reward of the godly will last. (Prov 11:18)

The cautious view that Proverbs takes of wealth has many facets. In Proverbs 13:11 it combines this caution with its conviction about the value of hard work:

Wealth from get-rich-quick schemes quickly disappears;
    wealth from hard work grows over time.

Elsewhere, Proverbs ponders how easily wealth can be accumulated by unethical means, and how inevitably it will turn and harm its owner:

Wealth created by a lying tongue
    is a vanishing mist and a deadly trap. (Prov 21:6)

A person who gets ahead by oppressing the poor
    or by showering gifts on the rich will end in poverty. (Prov 22:16)

The book of Proverbs is also clear that money will be of no avail for the things that are actually important in life.

Riches won't help on the day of judgment,
    but right living can save you from death. (Prov 11:4)

Exactly how to understand this "day of judgment" is debated. Is it simply a synonym for the day of death, or does it mean something more? For

Proverbs, the answer is unimportant. More important is that money cannot avert this day, so it is not as precious as right living.

The bottom line for Proverbs is that money is not the most important thing, and if it is achieved by dubious means, trouble may well result. All of this leads to the warning, given in a form that resembles closely the Egyptian wisdom we explored in chapter six:

> *Don't wear yourself out trying to get rich.*
> *Be wise enough to know when to quit.*
> *Just blink your eyes and wealth is gone,*
> *for it will sprout wings*
> *and fly away like an eagle. (Prov 23:4-5)*

Poverty is the result of injustice and oppression. It is wrong to suggest, as some do, that the book of Proverbs sees poverty as only and always resulting from laziness—or even from folly, generally understood. As we have seen, the proverbial form is never that sweeping or absolute; holding that it is can distort the book's overall message. Yes, laziness and other wrong-headed behaviors often result in poverty or something close to it. But not always.

When observing someone who is stuck in poverty, the wise person will study the situation before coming to any conclusions about causes or solutions. To do otherwise is to fall into the trap of Job's friends.

One thing the wise person might find—as Proverbs 13:23 points out— is unfairness:

> *A poor person's farm may produce much food,*
> *but injustice sweeps it all away.*

In keeping with the proverb form, the injustice is not made specific. Perhaps it is a crooked landlord. It may be a thief who steals the produce, or a government official who confiscates the farmer's goods. The proverb expresses a principle that may then be applied to other walks of life. The point, however, is clear: this poverty is not the result of laziness but of forces beyond the person's control.

Because Proverbs does not present a mechanistic view of the world or a simplistic view of the human condition, it can assert that a poor person may be more godly and wise than a rich person.

Better to be poor and godly
than rich and dishonest. (Prov 16:8)

Indeed, the poor find honor in the book of Proverbs. They are, in the most important sense, the equal of the rich:

The rich and poor have this in common:
The LORD made them both. (Prov 22:2)

Those with money must be generous. The book of Proverbs is sympathetic to the plight of the poor—mindful specifically of their needs as a group. As Proverbs 29:7 says:

The godly care about the rights of the poor;
the wicked don't care at all.

The king in particular is urged to care for the poor; in fact, doing so brings a blessing:

If a king judges the poor fairly,
his throne will last forever. (Prov 29:14)

Behind that blessing we are probably to hear an unspoken curse: If a king who is fair will have a long reign, then a king who is not fair will have a brief one. In Proverbs 28:27, this blessing and curse are expanded to everyone with means:

Whoever gives to the poor will lack nothing.
But curses will come on those who close their eyes to poverty.

Indeed, the book of Proverbs is not reticent about the rewards of generosity:

Give freely and become more wealthy;
be stingy and lose everything. (Prov 11:24)

But such an attitude appears paradoxical. How can you gain wealth by giving it away? Again, we need to remember that a proverb is not a guarantee, but rather a principle that is generally true. As if to reinforce this, the book of Proverbs is cautious about uncritical generosity. Proverbs 6:1-5 is typical of a major strand of teaching in the book that warns against giving loans to a friend who is in debt:

> *My child, if you have put up security for a friend's debt*
> *or agreed to guarantee the debt of a stranger—*
> *If you have trapped yourself by your agreement*
> *and are caught by what you said—*
> *follow my advice and save yourself,*
> *for you have placed yourself at your friend's mercy.*
> *Now swallow your pride;*
> *go and beg to have your name erased.*
> *Don't put it off; do it now!*
> *Don't rest until you do.*
> *Save yourself like a deer escaping from a hunter,*
> *like a bird fleeing from a net.*

These verses assume that the one who loans the money will be harmed if it is not returned. (Ex 22:25-27 forbids interest among fellow Israelites, so it is unlikely that the loans were made for financial gain, with the accompanying element of risk; the full amount was expected to be repaid.) But those who can give their money away and not need it back are urged to be generous:

> *Do not withhold good from those who deserve it*
> *when it's in your power to help them.*
> *If you can help your neighbor now, don't say,*
> *"Come back tomorrow, and then I'll help you."* (Prov 3:27-28)

Wisdom is better than wealth. Proverbs leaves us in no doubt that wealth is better than poverty, but is it the ultimate good? Absolutely not. We have already seen how Proverbs uses better-than forms to give us relative values:

> *Better to have little with fear for the LORD*
> *than to have great treasure with inner turmoil.* (Prov 15:16)

A bowl of soup with someone you love
   is better than steak with someone you hate. (Prov 15:17)

Better to be poor and godly
   than rich and dishonest. (Prov 16:8)

How much better to get wisdom than gold,
   and good judgment than silver! (Prov 16:16)

Better a dry crust eaten in peace
   than a great feast with conflict. (Prov 17:1)

Choose a good reputation over great riches,
   for it is better than silver and gold. (Prov 22:1)

Better to be poor and honest
   than rich and crooked. (Prov 28:6)

The first thing to notice about these passages is that they all are a ready admission that not everyone who is wise and godly will be wealthy or even live beyond a subsistence level. Proverbs recognizes that one can be poor and godly, or rich and a fool. Note also how many characteristics are more important than money. They include inner peace (Prov 15:16), relationships that are loving (Prov 15:17) and peaceful (Prov 17:1), honesty (Prov 16:8; 28:6), and a good reputation (Prov 22:1). These all flow from the even more central trait: wisdom (Prov 16:16)—also called the fear of the Lord (Prov 15:16), and godliness (Prov 16:8).

Wealth has limited value. Wisdom and its associated traits are much more important than money. To be sure, money can be helpful to people as they try to get on in life, but ultimately there is a limit to the value of material things. As we saw earlier,

Riches won't help you on the day of judgment,
   but right living can save you from death. (Prov 11:4)

Right living, associated throughout the book of Proverbs with wisdom, keeps a person from dangerous situations. One example (among many) is that right living means not sleeping with another man's wife. Such behavior, Proverbs warns, can lead to the most dire consequences at the hands of the woman's husband (Prov 6:34).

But wealth in some instances not only fails to help, it actually causes additional trouble. Consider, for instance, Proverbs 13:8:

> *The rich can pay a ransom for their lives,*
> *but the poor won't even get threatened.*

Here Proverbs acknowledges that money can get you released after you have been kidnapped. But the poor never even worry about being kidnapped because they have nothing the kidnappers would want. Riches can have other disadvantages, as when inappropriate ownership exposes the wealthy to scorn:

> *It isn't right for a fool to live in luxury*
> *or for a slave to rule over princes! (Prov 19:10)*

Money can bring yet additional problems—such as false friends, which seems to be behind the observation in Proverbs 14:20

> *The poor are despised even by their neighbors*
> *while the rich have many "friends."*

Perhaps these are some of the reasons, besides the stated one, that Agur, at the end of the book, offers the following prayer:

> *O God, I beg two favors from you;*
> *Let me have them before I die.*
> *First, help me never to tell a lie.*
> *Second, give me neither poverty nor riches!*
> *Give me just enough to satisfy my needs.*
> *For if I grow rich, I may deny you and say, "Who is the LORD"*
> *And if I am too poor, I may steal and thus insult God's holy name.*
> *(Prov 30:7-9)*

SUMMARY AND CONCLUSION

Proverbs has much to say about money, wealth, and poverty. To take one proverb, or even a group of related proverbs, as representing the viewpoint of the book would be quite misleading. Because the proverb form does not deal with the complexity of issues, a better approach (as I hope I've shown) is to list a number of different proverbs, then reflect on them, looking for how they group themselves and where they may clarify or nuance each other. The result, hopefully, will be a well-rounded and rich perspective, at least in terms of the book of Proverbs. For the biblical view on this subject, we would have to continue our study by looking elsewhere in Scripture.

Though I don't have the luxury of pursuing that broader subject here, you can begin the process with the questions for further reflection.

RELEVANT PASSAGES

Proverbs 3:9-10, 13-18; 6:6-11; 10:2, 4, 15-16, 22; 11:4, 16, 18, 24, 28; 13:7-8, 11, 18, 22-23; 14:20-21, 23-24; 15:6, 16-17; 16:8, 16; 17:1; 18:1, 23; 19:4, 10; 20:13; 21:5-6, 17, 20; 22:1, 2, 7, 16; 23:4; 28:3, 6, 11, 19-20, 22, 27; 29:7, 13-14; 30:7-9.

FOR FURTHER REFLECTION

1. Read Ecclesiastes 5:8-20. How does this passage relate to the message of Proverbs on wealth?
2. How does Ecclesiastes 7:11-12 relate to Proverbs?
3. Read James 5:1-6. What light does this throw on the biblical message on wealth?
4. What are your present attitudes about money? Did you learn anything new from Proverbs?
5. What does the message of Proverbs require from you today in terms of your actions and thinking about money?

FOR FURTHER READING

Washington, Harold C. *Wealth and Poverty in the Instructions of Amenemope and the Hebrew Proverbs*. Atlanta: Scholars Press, 1995.

Whybray, R. N. *Wealth and Poverty in the Book of Proverbs*. Sheffield, U.K.: JSOT Press, 1990.

ELEVEN

ON LOVING THE
RIGHT WOMAN

Up to this point in our study, we have carefully noted the subtle nuances of proverbs that instruct. With poverty and wealth, for instance, we described seven perspectives that on the surface often seemed in tension. We now know well that a proverb is not absolutely true in every situation. Its teaching or observation is generally true, but the wise must take into account the type of person with whom they are dealing and the circumstance before determining a proverb's relevance.

However, now we come to a major teaching in the book where we are left with little doubt about the right and wrong way: intimate sexual relationships. Proverbs has extensive teaching on loving the right woman and avoiding the woman who may seem so right but is so wrong. Note that the book only teaches men about proper relationships with women, not vice versa. As we have seen earlier, Proverbs in its original setting was addressed to young men. In the accompanying "excursus" I examine the question of why this perspective need not be an obstacle for women readers of Proverbs—or for men who are no longer "young."

The bulk of the book's instruction on women is found in Proverbs 1—9 in the form of lengthy discourses. Nonetheless, there are important proverbs in the second part of the book as well, including the powerful "Poem on the Virtuous Woman" that ends the book. We will spend significant time looking at that passage. However, since we cannot explore every relevant text, I have listed them all at the end of the chapter. We will focus on representative passages that give what I consider to be a well-rounded view of the book's teachings on relationships between men and women.

EXCURSUS: A WORD TO WOMEN READERS OF PROVERBS

I have tried to put myself, as a male, in the place of a woman who is reading Proverbs. Of course, that is not totally possible, in part because it requires stereotyping a woman's reaction to this teaching. Some female readers are by conviction sympathetic to the Bible's message and would have no problem accepting its male perspective. I would be saying to myself, *Fine, there are bad wives, but there are plenty of bad husbands as well. Why aren't women warned about the dangers of entering into a committed relationship with a bad man?*

Certainly the book of Proverbs recognizes that there are bad men as well as bad women. Both are described under the names of fool, scoffer or mocker. It is not much of a stretch to think that the book of Proverbs would frown on a wise woman, as well as wise man, marrying a fool. But we cannot escape the fact that Proverbs in its ancient setting is addressed to young men, and that Old Testament culture was male dominant. Even so, I would deny that there is any implication that women are somehow inherently inferior to men.

But in today's society, where we place—rightly, I believe—a premium on the equality of men and women, how do women read Proverbs? Indeed, how do they read Proverbs in the light of texts such as Galatians 3:28 that proclaims "there is neither . . . male or female. For you are all Christians—you are one in Christ Jesus"?

Quite simply, I believe modern readers are invited to read Proverbs by flipping the text to the other side of the relational equation. For example:

> It's better to live alone in the corner of an attic
> than with a quarrelsome husband in a lovely home. (Prov 21:9)

Isolated from the rest of Scripture, Proverbs addresses young men. Once it is included within the broader sweep of Scripture, a fuller application may be sought. After all, though individual biblical books are addressed to specific audiences at the time of their writing, the canon of Scripture is directed to all God's people. Jeremiah, for instance, addressed his prophetic oracles to the generation of Judeans who lived just before the Babylonian captivity. But do his divinely inspired warnings about sin, impending judgment, and the need for repentance apply only to that time and those people? No, they extend beyond to us today who are not Judeans, but perhaps American or British, Chinese or Korean. So also, we read Proverbs in the light of our modern culture, and if that culture has a different perception of men's and women's roles that the writer of Proverbs had, we read those words in the light of this different perception.

INSTRUCTION 1: AVOID IMMORAL WOMEN

As the father instructs his son in the first nine chapters, there is really one teaching that prevails: avoid immoral women. Proverbs 2:16-22; 3:13-18; 4:4-9; 6:20-35, and the entirety of chapters 5 and 7 are occupied with this theme. The father pulls out all of his stops to bombard his son with this warning. After all, as he points out to his son, the consequences of this foolish act are dire. After this major emphasis, it is a bit surprising, perhaps, to see how little attention is given to the subject in the second part of the book (only Prov 22:14; 23:26-28; 31:2). Indeed, the relevant proverbs simply reinforce the teaching of the discourses in the first part of the book.

Who are these women that young men are told to avoid? There are two types: the prostitute and the promiscuous wife. These women, in Hebrew, are referred to as "strange" (*zara*, translated "immoral woman" in NLT) and "foreign" (*nokriyya*; translated "promiscuous woman" in NLT). They are strange and foreign because they act outside the bounds of law and social convention, seeking sexual liaisons outside of marriage.

Sleeping with a prostitute or another person's wife is always wrong, but Proverbs sees a definite difference between the two. That difference involves the practical consequences that flow from these actions. This point is made in Proverbs 6:24-35. After a lengthy admonition to listen to the teaching, instructions and warnings of the parents, the father continues:

> *It will keep you from the immoral woman ('eset ra'),*
> *from the smooth tongue of the promiscuous woman.*
> *Don't lust for her beauty.*
> > *Don't let her coy glances seduce you.*
> *For a prostitute will bring you to poverty,*
> > *but sleeping with another man's wife will cost you your life.*
> *Can a man scoop a flame into his lap*
> > *and his clothes not catch on fire?*
> *Can he walk on hot coals*
> > *and not blister his feet?*
> *So it is with the man who sleeps with another man's wife.*
> > *He who embraces her will not go unpunished.*
> *Excuses might be found for a thief*
> > *who steals because he is starving.*
> *But even if he is caught, he must pay back seven times what he stole,*
> > *even if he has to sell everything in his house.*
> *But the man who commits adultery is an utter fool,*
> > *for he destroys himself.*
> *He will be wounded and disgraced.*
> > *His shame will never be erased.*
> *For the woman's jealous husband will be furious,*
> > *and he will show no mercy when he takes revenge.*
> *He will accept no compensation,*
> > *nor be satisfied with a payoff of any size.*

Again, the father is not saying that it is all right to have intercourse with a prostitute but not with a wife. He is saying that both are wrong, but the potential penalties are such that sleeping with a prostitute may impoverish a man, but sleeping with another man's wife may result in death at the hands of a jealous husband.

The argument can be made that these practical consequences reflect the customs of the day and are no longer valid. Indeed, women (wives) today have more recourses than did ancient Israelite women. Today, if a man sleeps with a prostitute, the consequences could be just as dire as sleeping with another man's wife (though in the latter instance, two marriage covenants are broken). Another difference between today and antiquity might be that today the prostitute herself is more likely to be married. In any case, sleeping with a wife or a prostitute is wrong, but the consequences of sleeping with the former are potentially more dangerous.

So why do it? The answer to that question explains why so much teaching is devoted to this subject: The temptation is great. The father does not try to minimize the temptation to the young man; on the surface it is an act that is hard to resist.

Interestingly, the most often cited reason for this temptation is the woman's speech. Her words to the man are flattering and seductive (Prov 2:16; 7:5). She wants the man and knows how to appeal to him. The immoral woman's mouth is attractive both for its sensuality and for uttering words that men like to hear. Probably both meanings are behind the warning in Proverbs 22:14:

> The mouth of an immoral woman is a dangerous trap;
> those who make the LORD angry will fall into it.

But it is not just the words of the woman that are tempting, it is also her body that she makes available to him. Proverbs 7 is the longest narrative concerning the seduction of a young man. It talks about how foolish a young man is to put himself in the way of temptation by going near the immoral woman's house. Not only does he hear her seductive words, he sees that she is "seductively dressed" (Prov 7:10). He is also captivated by her pleasant smells and the possibility of embrace.

Yet even though death is the result, the temptation is great. How can it be avoided? This question awaits answer in the following sections. However, by way of preview, I will simply point out that the best defense is a strong offense. Love your wife and develop a relationship with the most important Woman of all: Wisdom herself. We will begin with Proverbs' teaching about cultivating a relationship with one's wife.

INSTRUCTION 2: CULTIVATE A STRONG RELA-TIONSHIP WITH YOUR WIFE

Drink water from your own cistern,
  running water from your own well.
Should your springs overflow in the streets,
  your streams of water in the public squares?
Let them be yours alone,
  never to be shared with strangers.
May your fountain be blessed,
  and may you rejoice in the wife of your youth.
A loving doe, a graceful deer—
  may her breasts satisfy you always,
  may you ever be captivated by her love.
Why be captivated, my son, by an adulteress?
  Why embrace the bosom of another man's wife? (Prov 5:15-20 NIV)

Proverbs here turns the young man's attention away from the strange, foreign women who seem so enticing, and toward his own wife. There is a proper channel for youthful male sexual energy, and it is within the legal structure of marriage. Though there is not a hint of literary connection with Genesis 2, it is clear that this viewpoint is consistent with the idea that sex is part-and-parcel of the intimate relationship instituted at that time. Notice the exclusivity that is inherent in the man's hymnic response to the creation of the woman and in the words of explanation that follow:

"At last!" Adam exclaimed. "She is part of my own flesh and bone! She will be called 'woman,' because she was taken out of a man."
  This explains why a man leaves his father and mother and is joined to his wife, and the two are united into one. Now, although Adam and his wife were both naked, neither of them felt any shame. (Gen 2:23-25)

The practice of multiple wives and concubines that follows in the biblical story, though divinely condoned (Ex 21:7-11), is a step back from this ideal. A man's sexual energy is to be focused on one and only one woman, but in particular he is not to get involved with a woman with whom he has no legal relationship (the prostitute and the woman married to another man).

Proverbs 5 describes sexuality by using images that were well known to ancient Near Eastern readers. The "cistern" and the "well" suggest a vagina wet with sexual anticipation. The fountain image does as well. We can see another example of this in the Song of Songs, the Bible's most sensual of love poems. Specifically, we think of Song 4:12-15:

> *You are my private garden, my treasure, my bride,*
> *a secluded spring, a hidden fountain.*
> *Your thighs shelter a paradise of pomegranates and rare spices—*
> *henna with nard,*
> *nard with saffron,*
> *aromatic cane and cinnamon,*
> *every kind of fragrant wood,*
> *myrrh and aloes,*
> *and every other lovely spice.*
> *You are a garden spring,*
> *a well of fresh water*
> *streaming down from Lebanon's mountains.*[1]

On the other hand the overflowing springs and the streams of water of Proverbs 5:16 seem to refer to the man's sexuality, suggesting his ejaculate. The rhetorical question asks whether these should be shared broadly ("in the streets" and "in the public squares"). No, they should not; they should never be shared with strangers.

The text goes on and describes the man's wife and her body, again in language similar to the Song. She is a loving doe, a graceful deer. That the man should find satisfaction in her breasts alone is reminiscent of the man's speech in Song 7:6-9:

> *Oh, how beautiful you are!*
> *How pleasing, my love, how full of delights!*
> *You are slender like a palm tree,*
> *and your breasts are like its clusters of fruit.*
> *I said, "I will climb the palm tree*
> *and take hold of its fruit."*

May your breasts be like grape clusters,
  and the fragrance of your breath like apples.
May your kisses be as exciting as the best wine,
  flowing gently over lips and teeth.

Thus, the father presents the son with the first line of defense against the temptations of the strange, foreign woman: a healthy sexual relationship with his own wife. While a relationship with the strange woman leads to death, the relationship with one's wife leads to life.

INSTRUCTION 3: THE JOYS OF A GOOD WIFE

Proverbs understands that a good wife is one of the most important things in life. The first part of Proverbs 12:4 is indicative of this when it says, "a worthy wife is a crown for her husband." According to 14:1, her work is constructive for home life: "a wise woman builds her home." This verse, of course, does not imply that she is an architect, but rather that she constructs good relationships within the family. Accordingly, a good wife is something that only the Lord can provide:

The man who finds a wife finds a treasure;
  he receives a gift from the LORD. (Prov 18:22)

Indeed, in a subtle allusion to the sexual act—presumably, considering the canonical context, within marriage—Proverbs 30:18-20 lists the intimate relationship between a man and a woman as one of the most amazing things on earth:

There are three things that amaze me—
  no, four things I do not understand:
how an eagle glides through the sky,
  how a snake slithers on a rock,
  how a ship navigates through the ocean,
  how a man loves a woman.

This is contrasted with the sexuality of an adulterous woman, which also mystifies the writers: "Equally amazing is how an adulterous woman can satisfy her sexual appetite, shrug her shoulders, and then say, 'What's wrong with that?'" (Prov 30:20).

The most complete statement concerning the good wife comes in the magnificent poem that ends the book (Prov 31:10-31). It describes what may only be called the ideal woman or wife:

Who can find a virtuous and capable wife?
   She is more precious than rubies.
Her husband can trust her,
   and she will greatly enrich his life.
She brings him good, not harm,
   all the days of her life.
She finds wool and flax
   and busily spins it.
She is like a merchant's ship,
   bringing her food from afar.
She gets up before dawn to prepare breakfast for her household
   and plan the day's work for her servant girls.
She goes to inspect a field and buys it;
   with her earnings she plants a vineyard.
She is energetic and strong,
   a hard worker.
She makes sure her dealings are profitable;
   her lamp burns late into the night.
Her hands are busy spinning thread,
   her fingers twisting fiber.
She extends a helping hand to the poor
   and opens her arms to the needy.
She has no fear of winter for her household,
   for everyone has warm clothes.
She makes her own bedspreads.
   She dresses like royalty in gowns of fine cloth.
Her husband is well known at the city gates,
   where he sits with the other civic leaders.
She makes belted linen garments
   and sashes to sell to the merchants.
She is clothed with strength and dignity,
   and she laughs without fear of the future.

When she speaks, her words are wise,
and she gives instructions with kindness.
She carefully watches everything in her household
and suffers nothing from laziness.
Her children stand and bless her.
Her husband praises her:
"There are many virtuous and capable women in the world,
but you surpass them all!"
Charm is deceptive, and beauty does not last;
but a woman who fears the LORD will be greatly praised.
Reward her for all she has done.
Let her deeds publicly declare her praise.

This poem is a description of an ideal wife from a male point of view. The perspective is how this woman enhances the life of her husband. Again, the idea is to extol the wife in order to keep the husband from pursuing promiscuous women. As opposed to the latter, the virtuous and capable woman of Proverbs 31 exerts her efforts toward building her house and may thus also be seen as a filling out the details of the proverb we observed in 14:1.

The description is apparently that of an ideal woman. After reading of this multitalented woman, one wonders whether the opening question "Who can find a virtuous and capable woman?" was intended to be answered with a "No one." The poet, then, may be creating an ideal for which to strive.

A few observations on this poem will enrich our reading. One of its most curious features is the occasional use of military terminology. Unfortunately, this is usually completely submerged in English translation. The very word "virtuous" (*hayil*) is connected to military prowess.[2] Where the NLT says "she will greatly enrich his life" (v. 11), the Hebrew text may be more literally understood as "he will not lack plunder" (*wĕ salal lo' yehsar*). The "plunder" that the wife brings her husband will indeed enrich his life. Perhaps life's struggles here are envisioned as a war, and the woman as an active and successful participant in taming life's chaos.

Another of the dominant themes throughout the poem is the woman's boundless energy. It is hard to believe that any single person could ever accomplish as much as this ideal woman, and perhaps the description is meant as a composite sketch. In any case, this woman is described not only as a warrior but also as a merchant ship that brings produce to port, namely her home. She also is active in commercial endeavors, not to speak of philanthropy toward the needy.

Not only her actions are praised, but also her qualities of mind and attitude. She is fearless about the future, wise and kind. This woman has nothing at all to do with laziness.

The emphasis at the end of the poem, as one might expect, is not on beauty or charm, but on the woman's fear of the Lord. Indeed, this woman is the epitome of wisdom. She is the human embodiment of God's wisdom; a flesh-and-blood personification of Woman Wisdom.

We will turn to this aspect in just a moment, but first we must consider the human opposite of the virtuous woman. What does the book of Proverbs say about the bad wife?

INSTRUCTION 4: THE AGONY OF A BAD CHOICE

Not all wives are as supportive as the virtuous woman of Proverbs 31. Some are not even close. Proverbs makes some of its most witty observations in regard to a wife who is not a help but a hindrance to her husband. Indeed, the importance of this subject is underlined by its repetition throughout the book. Working our way in like manner, we begin at 11:22:

A beautiful woman who lacks discretion
  is like a gold ring in a pig's snout.

Here we note Proverbs' relative values concerning a good woman/wife. As we heard at the end of Proverbs 31, "beauty does not last." However, beauty is what often attracts a man in the first place and can serve as a trap. For one thing, a lack of discretion can spoil a woman's beauty. While looking at the gold ring, we don't see the pig. Lack of discretion can lead to all kinds of problems, such as illegitimate relationships or misuse of resources—things that undermine wise living in a difficult world.

We saw that 12:4 began with the image of a worthy wife who is a crown for her husband; here we note the antithetical second part of the verse:

But a disgraceful woman is like cancer in his bones.

A poor match with the wrong woman can eat away at a person like an internal disease ("rot" in the Hebrew; "cancer" in the NLT). These observations are clearly intended to warn the young man to avoid such entanglements. Again, we saw in 14:1 that the first colon spoke of the constructive effect of a wise woman. What about the foolish woman? She "tears [her house] down with her own hands."

As memorable as these proverbs are through their use of vivid images and biting sarcasm, none are more striking than the "better-than" proverbs that rank singleness over a bad match:

*It's better to live alone in the corner of an attic
    than with a quarrelsome wife in a lovely home. (Prov 21:9; 25:24)*

*It's better to live alone in the desert
    than with a quarrelsome, complaining wife. (Prov 21:19)*

These verses are complemented by the expanded proverb found in 27:15-16:

*A quarrelsome wife is as annoying
    as constant dripping on a rainy day.
Stopping her complaints is like trying to stop the wind
    or trying to hold something with greased hands.*

INSTRUCTION 5: HUMAN ECHOES OF DIVINE REALITIES

The reader of Proverbs is confronted with a choice in regard to women on two levels. In this chapter, we have focused on the choice between the wife and the promiscuous woman. Though a wife may be quarrelsome or annoying (and such observations may serve the purpose of warning the young man about too hasty a marriage), there is never a suggestion that the man should leave or abandon her. On the other hand, no matter how tempting a liaison with an immoral woman may be, it is to be avoided at all costs. A relationship with a wife leads to life, but death may well result from consorting with another woman, particularly some other man's wife.

By now this dynamic should have a familiar ring. In chapter three we saw that Proverbs 1—9 calls the young male reader to make a decision between Woman Wisdom and Woman Folly. As we unpacked those images, we recognized that the former represented Yahweh's Wisdom, indeed a relationship with Yahweh himself. Woman Folly, on the other hand, stood for the idols that competed for the men's affections.

Now we can see how the wife is a human reflection of Woman Wisdom and the promiscuous woman is a human reflection of Woman Folly. To unite with the former pair leads to life, but to unite with the latter pair results in death.

The father, therefore, urges his son to develop an intimate relationship with Woman Wisdom, and he uses sexual language to make his point:

Wisdom is a tree of life to those who embrace her;
  happy are those who hold her tightly. (Prov 3:18)

Don't turn your back on wisdom, for she will protect you.
  Love her, and she will guard you.
Getting wisdom is the wisest thing you can do!
  And whatever else you do, develop good judgment.
If you prize wisdom, she will make you great.
  Embrace her and she will honor you.
She will place a love wreath on your head;
  she will protect you with a beautiful crown. (Prov 4:6-9)

Indeed, a strong relationship with Woman Wisdom, just as we saw above in terms of a wife, is a defense against an illegitimate union with a promiscuous woman.

Wisdom will save you from the immoral woman,
  from the seductive words of the promiscuous woman. (Prov 2:16)

How will Wisdom accomplish this? In the first place, a relationship with Woman Wisdom is a cipher for a relationship with Yahweh. One who embraces Wisdom fears Yahweh and therefore will follow his commands, including the one not to commit adultery. Second, the one who gets Wisdom will also use common sense and discern the true nature of the situation. Relating to a beautiful but strange woman may seem so right, so pleasurable on the surface, but there is a world of trouble in store for the one who does it. Only the fool stumbles blindly into such a situation.

CONCLUSION

As we began the chapter, so we end. Though communicated in an intriguing manner, the book's teaching about women is quite straightforward. Avoid the strange woman, the human reflection of Woman Folly, and embrace the virtuous woman, who represents Woman Wisdom on a human level. For women who are reading Proverbs, the reverse applies. Avoid the strange man, the man who is a fool, but embrace the man who is virtuous. The consequences for both are the same: life or death.

RELEVANT PASSAGES

Proverbs 2:16-22; 3:13-18; 4:4-9; 5:1-23; 6:20-35; 7:1-27; 8:1-36; 9:1-18; 11:16, 22; 12:4, 22; 14:1; 21:9, 19; 22:14; 23:26-28; 25:24; 27:15-16; 29:3; 30:18-23; 31:2-3, 10-31

FOR FURTHER REFLECTION

1. What do you think of the way that Proverbs evaluates a "good" and "bad" woman/wife?
2. Men, assess your attitude toward women in the light of the book of Proverbs.
3. What adjustments might women make as they reread these passages but substitute husband or man for wife/woman?
4. Women, assess your attitude toward men in the light of the book of Proverbs.
5. What does this teaching have to do with theology anyway?

TWELVE

WISE WORDS,
FOOLISH WORDS

The adage "Sticks and stones may break my bones, but words will never hurt me" may be clever, but it was not formulated by a sage. According to Proverbs, words are life-bringing or death-dealing; they are certainly not harmless. Words are critical to the wise person as is indicated by the extensive number of proverbs dealing with the subject (see the list at the end of this chapter).

After all, Proverbs is a book of advice on how to navigate life successfully, and advice comes in the form of words, both written and oral. Great care is taken in the book not only with what is said but with how the message is communicated. Indeed, the sages who produced the book saved some of their most striking images to describe and advise their students concerning the difference between wise and foolish speech.

WORDS AND THE HEART

One reason why words are so important to the wise men and women of Israel is because they understood that words reflect the condition of the heart. Proverbs 12:23, for instance, observes:

> The wise don't make a show of their knowledge,
>   but [the hearts of][1] fools broadcast their foolishness.

Proverbs 16:23 speaks on the side of wisdom when it states:

From a wise mind [heart] comes wise speech;
the words of the wise are persuasive.

The connection between the character of wisdom and wise words is brought home forcefully by Proverbs 18:4:

Wise words are like deep waters;
wisdom flows from the wise like a bubbling brook.

The connection between words and heart also explains why occasionally these two words can appear in parallel to one another:

The words of the godly are like sterling silver;
the heart of a fool is worthless. (Prov 10:20)

On the other hand, the wise are warned to be aware that flattering words can hide a crooked heart:

Smooth words may hide a wicked heart,
just as a pretty glaze covers a clay pot. (Prov 26:23)

The glaze gives an attractive sheen to the plain surface of the pot, but it is only skin deep. As we will see, being careful with words is important because of the consequences. By way of anticipation, we can cite the extended proverb found in 26:24-26:

People may cover their hatred with pleasant words,
but they're deceiving you.
They pretend to be kind, but don't believe them.
Their hearts are full of many evils.
While their hatred may be concealed by trickery,
their wrongdoing will finally come to light for all to see.

Thus our suspicions are confirmed. Fools cannot hide their hearts forever. Their true nature will eventually emerge in all of its verbal ugliness.

WORDS AND REALITY

We have just seen that words reflect the reality of the speaker's heart.

Certainly it is possible for some people, temporarily, to cover up what is going on inside their personality, but not for long. On the other hand, the book of Proverbs understands that wise words match external reality, while foolish words distort the connection between the mind and the world.

This point is simply expressed in the straightforward words of Proverbs 12:17:

> *An honest witness tells the truth;*
> *a false witness tells lies.*

The truth conforms to reality; the lie twists it. The simplicity of these words reminds us that Proverbs comes from a time long before postmodernism's mischievous undermining of the connection between words and their referents.[2] (The book of Proverbs assumes that words can at least adequately represent reality outside of ourselves, and it would quite honestly consider much of the writings of contemporary postmodern authors as the babbling of fools.)

Again, as smooth words may hide a foolish heart, so a lie may temporarily stand for a truth. But the ultimate victory goes to those words that conform to the true nature of things:

> *Truthful words stand the test of time,*
> *but lies are soon exposed. (Prov 12:19)*

Wise people are accordingly warned to be careful that their speech reflects reality:

> *Spouting off before listening to the facts*
> *is both shameful and foolish. (Prov 18:13)*

All of this adds up to the importance of finding out whose words are true and whose are false:

> *The first to speak in court sounds right,*
> *but then comes cross-examination. (Prov 18:17)*

AN ANATOMY OF FALSE WORDS

The fool speaks words that are false in more than one way. They may misrepresent reality by exaggeration or simple falsehood. However, false words may be factually true, but spoken at an inappropriate time or with malicious intent.

In any case, these words mark the speaker as a fool. As a matter of fact, one of the strongest words for a fool in the book of Proverbs refers to bad speech: it is "mocker" or "scorner" *(lason* from the verbal root *lys)*. One who mocks uses language to hurt others, to laugh at or ridicule them. Indeed, according to a string of proverbs, foolish language has harm as its ultimate intention:

> *The godly are showered with blessings;*
> *   the words of the wicked conceal violent intentions. (Prov 10:6)*

> *The words of the wicked are like a murderous ambush,*
> *   but the words of the godly save lives. (Prov 12:6)*

> *Throw out the mocker, and fighting goes too.*
> *   quarrels and insults will disappear. (Prov 22:10)*

The last quoted proverb also reminds us that the harm of false words focuses on relationships. The words of fools don't bring people together; rather they tear them apart.

False words that destroy relationships can come in all kinds of guises. We will survey a few of the categories of foolish speech commented on by the book of Proverbs.

Lies. The largest category of foolish words in the book is the lie *(seqer* and *kezeb* are the most common Hebrew words). The lie misrepresents the truth; it deceives the hearer. The sages of Proverbs often comment on the importance of truth in the courtroom. Proverbs 14:5 makes the simple observation:

> *A truthful witness saves lives,*
> *   but a false witness breathes lies*

while 14:25 evaluates the difference in strong terms:

A truthful witness saves lives,
  but a false witness is a traitor.

God hates the liar, as we can see from the list in Proverbs 6:16-19 that places the deceiver in the context of shame:

There are six things the LORD hates—
  no, seven things he detests:
  haughty eyes,
  a lying tongue,
  hands that kill the innocent,
  a heart that plots evil,
  feet that race to do wrong,
  a false witness who pours out lies,
  a person who sows discord in a family.

God hates the liar (as do the godly [Prov 13:5]) because of the harm done to the other, as so powerfully expressed in Proverbs 25:18:

Telling lies about others
  is as harmful as hitting them with an ax,
  wounding them with a sword,
  or shooting them with a sharp arrow.

A lie harms in one of two ways. It misrepresents the past so the recipient acts on false knowledge, or it misrepresents the future (a deceptive promise) so the recipient depends on an agreed-upon condition that never materializes. Given the nature of the lie, it is not surprising that the fool gets caught in many arguments.

Arguments. As we will see below, the wise person does not avoid hard words when necessary. But the fool seems to pick fights just for the sake of fighting. Fools are people who like quarrels, and according to Proverbs 26:21 they are quick to get involved:

A quarrelsome person starts fights
  as easily as hot embers light charcoal or fire lights wood.

On the other hand, the sages' advice is for the wise to do their best not to get involved:

Interfering in someone else's argument
   is as foolish as yanking a dog's ears. (Prov 26:17)

Arguments disrupt relationships. There may be a time for a fight—that seems to be behind the contrary advice we examined in Proverbs 26:4 and 5—but it is wise to pick and choose which fights to take on.

Insult/Slander.

Hiding hatred makes you a liar;
   slandering others makes you a fool. (Prov 10:18)

If you insult your father or mother,
   the lamp of your life will be snuffed out. (Prov 20:20)

The fool may sometimes attack another person head-on, using words to make a malicious statement about character or actions or appearance. Again, it is not that the wise person only says nice things about another, but the intention of the fool in an insult or slander is only to hurt, belittle and demean the other. Thus relationship is once again destroyed.

Gossip/Rumor.

The gossip goes around telling secrets,
   but those who are trustworthy can keep a confidence. (Prov 11:13)

Rumors are dainty morsels
   that sink deep into one's heart. (Prov 18:8)

Rumors are negative reports about other people that are based on uncertain evidence. They are spread to injure the person, not to help. Gossip may ultimately turn out to be true, but that does not exonerate the person who speaks it to others. If true, then the report is being given to inappropriate people at an inappropriate time.

Interestingly, it is not only telling gossip or spreading rumor that is frowned on by Proverbs but also listening to it:

Wrongdoers eagerly listen to gossip;
   liars pay close attention to slander. (Prov 17:4)

Flattery/Bragging. Flattery and bragging, though different in many ways, both intentionally speak better than is warranted of another or oneself, and often with the similar purpose of self-promotion. One flatters by excessively complimenting others with the hidden purpose of getting something for oneself and even harming the person. The prime case of flattery is the promiscuous woman who wants to use the young man for her own purposes regardless of the harm that will come to his relationships and career:

> *She seduced him with her pretty speech*
> *and enticed him with her flattery.*
> *He followed her at once,*
> *like an ox going to the slaughter. (Prov 7:21-22)*

With flattery, appearances do not reflect reality:

> *Smooth words may hide a wicked heart,*
> *just as a pretty glaze covers a clay pot. (Prov 26:23)*

On the other hand, bragging presents a better picture of the speaker than is warranted. Even if one has accomplished great things, it is not proper to promote oneself:

> *Let someone else praise you, not your own mouth;*
> *a stranger, not your own lips. (Prov 27:2)*

Lies, deception, rumors, gossip, insults, slander, boasting, flattery—these all constitute the arsenal of foolish speech. Foolish people reflect the speech of their leader, Woman Folly, who lies and deceives to harm her hearers (Prov 9:13-18). The words of fools harm others and ultimately, at least, injure those who speak them as well. Before exploring this last point, though, we will consider the characteristics of wise speech.

AN ANATOMY OF WISE WORDS

As the words of fools reflect Woman Folly, so the words of the wise reflect Woman Wisdom, who states:

> *I speak the truth*
> *and detest every kind of deception.*

> *My advice is wholesome.*
>   *There is nothing devious or crooked in it.*
> *My words are plain to anyone with understanding,*
>   *clear to those with knowledge. (Prov 8:7-9)*

The words of the wise, therefore, are true and helpful. They heal rather than wound; they give life rather than death.

> *The words of the wise are a life-giving fountain;*
>   *the words of the wicked conceal violent intentions. (Prov 10:11)*

According to Proverbs, the words of the wise—again in contrast to those of evil people—are few and usually gentle. Indeed, there is a major strand of teaching in the book about the importance of silence.

> *Those who control their tongue will have a long life;*
>   *opening your mouth can ruin everything. (Prov 13:3)*

Silence can even mask the ignorance of fools according to Proverbs 17:28:

> *Even fools are thought to be wise when they keep silent;*
>   *with their mouths shut, they seem intelligent.*

One's words should be few, but also normally delivered gently.

> *Gentle words are a tree of life;*
>   *a deceitful tongue crushes the spirit. (Prov 15:4)*

> *Kind words are like honey—*
>   *sweet to the soul and healthy for the body. (Prov 16:24)*

On the other hand, when the occasion demands it the wise person knows how to deliver strong words, and the wise happily receive necessary correction to their behavior.

> *An open rebuke*
>   *is better than hidden love! (Prov 27:5)*

Thus, the differences between the speech of the wise and foolish could not be more opposite. It is the difference between truth and falsehood, deception and clarity, language in service of Woman Wisdom and language in service of Woman Folly. It is, therefore, not surprising that the consequences of these words are also opposite: life and death.

THE CONSEQUENCES OF WISE
AND FOOLISH WORDS

There are consequences of foolish speech that destroy others and of wise speech that build others up. Proverbs 18:21 puts the matter quite clearly:

> *The tongue can bring death or life;*
> *those who love to talk will reap the consequences. (Prov 18:21)*

Death is the end of the road for those who use their speech to hurt others. But before that come shame and disgrace:

> *Spouting off before listening to the facts*
> *is both shameful and foolish. (Prov 18:13)*

And it spells trouble as well:

> *The wicked are trapped by their own words,*
> *but the godly escape such trouble. (Prov 12:13)*

This last proverb is also indicative of the idea pervasive in the book of Proverbs, that the very speech of fools will harm and ultimately kill them. A handful of proverbs speak of the fool's words as a rod for beating them:

> *The proud talk of fools becomes a rod with which others beat them,*
> *but the words of the wise keep them safe. (Prov 14:3)*

These dire consequences for foolish speech are presented to warn the reader not to use speech to harm others and ultimately themselves. In the same way, constructive speech has its rewards, from the simple fact that "wise words will win you a good meal" (Prov 13:2) to the more serious observation that "those who control their tongue will have a long life" (Prov 13:3a).

IN CONCLUSION: JAMES ON CONTROLLING
THE TONGUE

In many ways the book of James is a New Testament wisdom book. One area of striking similarity to the book of Proverbs is its teaching on speech. James 3 is addressed to teachers in the church since their speech is particularly edifying or destructive to others. Through the striking metaphors of the bridle on a horse and a rudder on a ship, James points out that the tongue, though small, has a tremendous influence on the direction of one's life. Further, he says, a tiny spark can cause an incredibly damaging fire. The tongue is surprisingly hard to control, but control it one must.

Perhaps it is because of the difficulty of taming the tongue that James next turns to the source of true wisdom. Again, in the tradition of Proverbs this New Testament writer understands that wisdom is more than just good advice dependent on human resources; rather true wisdom comes "from heaven" (Jas 3:17). Such wisdom "will plant seeds of peace and reap a harvest of goodness" (Jas 3:18).

RELEVANT PASSAGES

Proverbs 6:16-19, 24; 7:21; 8:6-9, 13; 10:6, 11, 13-14, 18-21, 30, 32; 11:9, 11-13; 12:6, 13-14, 17-19, 22-23; 13:2-3, 5; 14:3, 5, 25; 15:1-2, 4, 7, 23; 16:13, 23-24; 17:4, 7, 20, 28; 18:4, 6-8, 13, 17, 20-21; 19:5, 9; 20:15, 19-20; 21:23, 28; 22:10; 25:9-11, 18, 20, 23, 25; 26:4-7, 9, 17, 20-26, 28; 27:1-2, 5, 14-16; 29:5, 8-9, 11, 15, 19; 30:10-11, 17, 32; 31:8

FOR FURTHER REFLECTION

1. What are some of the common characteristics of wise words? foolish words?
2. Why do words have such power to encourage or devastate?
3. In the light of the categories provided by Proverbs, reflect on the words you used today and yesterday.
4. Do you think you speak too much? too little? Why?
5. Think about how others react to your words. Do they achieve their intended effect?

6. Choose one of the following topics: decision-making/planning; anger; pride; bribery/gifts; alcohol; friendship; relationship with neighbors. Collect the appropriate texts in Proverbs and reflect on the content.

PRINCIPLES FOR READING
THE BOOK OF PROVERBS

everal principles, derived from our exploration of how to read Proverbs, can help you gain the most from reading the book of Proverbs. But they should be used only after working through the chapters we have already covered—and which I have indicated in parentheses after each principle.

1. Keep in mind the structure of the whole book of Proverbs as you read any part of it. In particular, make sure you read any passage of the book in the light of the imagery concerning the path and the two women that is developed in Proverbs 1—9 and reaches its climax in Proverbs 8—9 (chapters two and three).

2. Reflect on the parallelism of a proverb by asking how the second colon sharpens or intensifies the thought of the first (chapter four).

3. Identify the imagery in a passage, then unpack it by asking how the two things compared are similar and how they are different (chapter four).

4. Think about the source of the wisdom of a passage. Does it come from observation, experience, tradition, revelation or any combination of these sources (chapter five)?

5. Is the passage an observation, a bit of advice, a warning, a reflection,

or some other kind of teaching (chapter five)?

6. Since proverbs are not true in any and every circumstance, ask under what circumstances the proverb may or may not apply to a situation (chapter five). How can you tell?

7. Does the proverb mention or imply a reward or punishment that will result from obedience or disobedience (chapter seven)?

8. If the passage is addressed to a young man, ask how it applies to you (chapter two).

9. Using a commentary, study the Near Eastern background of the passage you are considering (chapter six). (See the list of suggested commentaries in appendix two or *The IVP Bible Background Commentary: Old Testament* by John H. Walton, Victor H. Matthews and Mark Chavalas [Downers Grove, Ill.: InterVarsity Press, 2000].)

10. When doing a topical study, read through the book of Proverbs and pinpoint the relevant verses. Group them together, then study each group (chapters ten through twelve).

11. Try to identify biblical stories or characters who may illustrate the truthfulness of the proverb(s) you are studying (chapter eight).

12. Does the New Testament address the topic or teaching of the passage you are studying (chapter twelve)?

13. Think of Christ as the fulfillment of wisdom and how he might illustrate the wisdom of the passage you are reading (chapter nine).

FINAL WORD

God has given Proverbs as a gift to his people, and its importance has not diminished by virtue of its antiquity. Life continues to be complicated; every day has issues both small and great. Not a week goes by without an important decision to be made or action to take that affects our most important relationships and our personal well-being.

Proverbs can help us navigate those perilous waters. It gives us advice and imparts observations so we might live life with maximum enjoyment and effectiveness. In this way, Proverbs could well be characterized as a self-improvement book.

But this would be a mistake. Proverbs is so much more than a collection of well-crafted insights into living. It is a thoroughly theological book, confronting us from the very beginning with the most fundamental of choices: What is or should be the driving force of my life? Will I enter a relationship with Wisdom or Folly? with God or idols? A particular choice faces the Christian reader: In light of the New Testament's teaching on the nature of wisdom, is Jesus Christ, the epitome of God's wisdom, at the center of my life's decisions and actions?

AUTHORSHIP AND DATE
OF THE BOOK OF PROVERBS

Some may be surprised that I have reserved this discussion for the very end of the book and even placed it in an appendix. I did this not because my viewpoint is particularly controversial or I think the topic is uninteresting or unimportant. Rather, I did it because this is a book about how to read the book of Proverbs, and if we are quite honest, the authorship and date of the book have little or no impact on our interpretation of it. Nonetheless, many readers will have questions about this matter, so we turn our attention to what we can know about the book's composition.

AUTHORSHIP

Many people think that the authorship of Proverbs is established in the first verse: "These are the proverbs of Solomon, David's son, king of Israel" (Prov 1:1). As we read on, though, the issue becomes much more complex. Other sections are marked by captions that seem to attribute authorship to others. For instance, 22:17 and 24:23 mention a group called simply "the wise"; 30:1 and 31:1 mention two unknown kings named Agur and Lemuel respectively; 10:1 and 25:1 mention Solomon again, but the latter also ascribes some type of role to the "advisers of King Hezekiah of Judah." Thus the question of authorship seems much more complex after a complete reading of the book.

Indeed, there is quite a variety of opinion about the compositional history of the book. The extremes are predictable. Very conservative scholars argue that Solomon authored the parts directly attributed to him and also collected and presented the work of the other wisdom figures periodically named in the book.[1] On the other hand, there are scholars who argue that nothing in the book can be directly associated with Solomon and that his association with the book is the result of his legendary wisdom.[2]

The majority of present-day scholars limit Solomon's contribution to 10:1—22:16 and 25:1—29:27, sections that constitute a major—and perhaps the earliest—portion of the book. Thus it is certainly appropriate for the first verse to identify Solomon as the main contributor and the initiator of the anthology. After all, his connection with biblical wisdom is a major theme of the historical narrative in the book of Kings. He prays for and receives wisdom from God (1 Kings 3:1-15), then demonstrates that wisdom in a practical case (1 Kings 3:16-28). His wisdom far surpasses that of anyone else in the world (1 Kings 4:29-31), amazing even the Queen of Sheba, who travels a long distance to confirm what she has heard about him (1 Kings 10:1-23). His wisdom led to a prodigious production of proverbs; 1 Kings 4:32 declares that three thousand are attributed to him.

Nothing much is known about the other authors named in the book. The names Agur and Lemuel occur only here and with scant additional information. The "wise" are anonymous, though their designation may indicate that they were professional scholars perhaps serving the court.

The only other group named in the book are the aforementioned advisors to King Hezekiah. While early Jewish tradition may have ascribed authorship of the book to them ("Hezekiah and his company wrote the Proverbs," *Baba Bathra* 15a), Proverbs 25:1 clearly gives them a scribal and perhaps editorial role.

DATE

As any anthology, Proverbs is composed of material written over a period of time. We do not know how long, because there are anonymous sections of the book as well as named authors about whom we know nothing. We are on firm ground only with Solomon (tenth century B.C.) and the men of Hezekiah (ca. 700 B.C.). Since the work of the latter is limited to one small portion of the book, it is reasonable to infer that there was an even later editorial stage that arranged the entire book and provided the short introduction (Prov 1:1-7). The exact date of this final editing is not known.

It is virtually impossible to date, even relatively, the writing of the other parts of the book. It is often argued that 1:8—9:18 is the latest part of the book. Scholars cite as evidence the more complex and longer style (Proverbs 2 is a single sentence, according to some), the more explicitly religious perspective (and specifically the personification of wisdom) and the supposed lateness of some words (particularly *'etun,* "linens," in Proverbs 7:16).[3] The first two arguments, style and perspective,[4] have been resisted by von Rad, who believes they are a figment of the form critic's imagination.[5] Arguments regarding the lateness of the words run into the difficulties of any linguistic argument for dating—the evidence is not adequate to give any certainty. Kayatz has suggested more recently that the differences between 1:8—9:18 and the rest of the book have more to do with style than chronology.[6]

COMMENTARIES ON THE
BOOK OF PROVERBS

The following are all excellent; which one you buy depends on what you are looking for, since not every commentary can address every aspect of the book. Also, the various commentaries come from different theological and methodological perspectives.

Aitken, Kenneth T. *Proverbs*. Philadelphia: Westminster Press, 1986. Daily study Bible. An interesting feature of this readable commentary is the topical ordering of the material in Proverbs 10 and following.

Clifford, Richard J. *Proverbs*. Old Testament Library Series. Louisville, Ky.: John Knox/Westminster, 1999. This commentary puts more emphasis on text criticism, philology and ancient Near Eastern background than some of the others listed here. His exposition of the meaning of the Hebrew is a little less substantial than that of other commentaries, but it is still very good.

Fox, Michael V. *Proverbs 1-9*. Anchor Bible Commentaries. Garden City, N.Y.: Doubleday, 2000. This is an excellent commentary both because the series allows more space than other commentaries and because Fox is a master interpreter. The only drawback is that it covers just the first nine chapters of Proverbs. Hopefully, we will not have to wait too long for the rest of the commentary to appear.

Kidner, Derek. *Proverbs*. Tyndale Old Testament Commentary Series. Downers Grove, Ill.: InterVarsity Press, 1964. This small commentary is packed with helpful insight and comments on the text. It is exegetically sensitive and theologically helpful.

Longman, Tremper, III. *Proverbs*. Grand Rapids, Mich.: Baker, forthcoming.

McKane, William. *Proverbs: A New Approach*. Old Testament Library. Philadelphia: Westminster Press, 1970. This commentary is over thirty years old but still retains its value—in spite of its many critical conclusions.

Murphy, Roland E. *Proverbs*. Word Biblical Commentary Series. Nashville: Thomas Nelson, 1998. Murphy is a preeminent interpreter of wisdom literature.

Perdue, Leo G. *Proverbs*. Interpretation Series. Louisville, Ky.: John Knox Press, 2000. This commentary focuses on the literary, structural, ethical and theological issues of the book of Proverbs. Its perspective is critical but moderately applied; a source of many good insights.

Ross, Allen P. "Proverbs." In *The Expositor's Bible Commentary*. Edited by F. Gaebelein. Grand Rapids, Mich.: Zondervan, 1991. This commentary is excellent and one of the best in its series. Since it is bound with Willem VanGemeren's excellent Psalms commentary, it is definitely worth having.

Van Leeuwen, Raymond. "Proverbs." In *The New Interpreter's Bible*. Nashville: Abingdon, 1997. 5:19-264. This commentary exposits the text and also reflects on it theologically. Written from a progressive evangelical perspective, it is one of the best commentaries on Proverbs.

Waltke, Bruce. *Proverbs*. New International Commentary on the Old Testament Series. Grand Rapids, Mich.: Eerdmans, forthcoming.

NOTES

Chapter 1: Why Read Proverbs?
[1]See the discussion of the superscription in appendix 1.
[2]Daniel Goleman, *Emotional Intelligence* (New York: Bantam, 1995).
[3]Ibid., p. xii.
[4]Ibid., p. 34.
[5]For additional insight into these and other words related to the wisdom idea in Proverbs, see the excellent discussion in Michael V. Fox, *Proverbs 1-9*, Anchor Bible (Garden City, N.Y.: Doubleday, 2000), pp. 28-38.
[6]For a defense of the translation accepted here, see Tremper Longman III, *Proverbs* (Grand Rapids, Mich.: Baker, forthcoming).

Chapter 2: Walking on the Path of Life
[1]Or "narratee," using Adele Berlin's terminology; see *Poetics and Interpretation of Biblical Narrative* (Sheffield, U.K.: Almond, 1983), pp. 52-54.
[2]The translation is from Miriam Lichtheim, *Ancient Egyptian Literature* (Berkeley: University of California Press, 1975), 1:58.
[3]I am using the New Living Translation, which is a gender-inclusive version and thus renders "my son" as "my child" except in those places in Proverbs 5—7 where the son is being warned about promiscuous women.

Chapter 3: Woman Wisdom or Folly—Which Will It Be?
[1]Note that I do not cite Proverbs 9:7-12 here. Scholars debate their connection with the rest of the chapter, most concluding that these verses were added later and are not integrally related to the rest of the text. However, for a significant and largely persuasive counter-argument see R. Byargeon, "The Structure and Significance of Prov. 9:7-12," *JETS* 40 (1997): 367-76.

[2]See Tremper Longman III, *Immanuel in Our Place: Seeing Christ in Israel's Worship* (Phillipsburg, N.J.: P & R, 2001).

[3]This conclusion is controversial among biblical scholars. Most will admit that Woman Wisdom stands for Yahweh's wisdom, but hesitate to take the next step and say that she represents Yahweh himself. However, such denials do not take into account the location of her house and conversely the house of Woman Folly.

Chapter 4: What Exactly Is a Proverb—and How Does It Work?

[1]For more detail than offered here, see my earlier book *How to Read the Psalms* (Downers Grove, Ill.: InterVarsity Press, 1988), pp. 95-110.

[2]See James Kugel, *The Idea of Biblical Poetry: Parallelism and Its History* (New Haven, Conn.: Yale University Press, 1981); Robert Alter, *The Art of Biblical Poetry* (New York: Basic Books, 1985).

[3]See Raymond Van Leeuwen, "Proverbs," in *A Complete Literary Guide to the Bible*, ed. Leland Ryken and Tremper Longman III (Grand Rapids, Mich.: Zondervan, 1993), p. 261.

[4]I have benefited greatly from Leland Ryken's description of imagery and symbolism in Ryken, James C. Wilhoit and Tremper Longman III, eds., *Dictionary of Biblical Imagery* (Downers Grove, Ill.: InterVarsity Press, 1998), pp. xiii-xiv. However, I use *imagery* as a synonym for *symbolism* in a way that he does not. He, like me, uses *symbolism* as a synonym for *metaphor* and *simile*.

[5]It may be true that even in the Old Testament period this image was tamed by frequent use. However, this does not hurt my point that images are coined to attract the reader's attention by shock value.

[6]For an excellent guide to the details of Hebrew poetry, see Wilfred G. E. Watson, *Classical Hebrew Poetry* (Sheffield, U.K.: JSOT Press, 1984).

Chapter 5: Are Proverbs Always True?

[1]For important studies that make this point, see Barbara Kirshenblatt-Gimblett, "Toward a Theory of Proverb Meaning," *Proverbium* 22 (1973): 823, and Carole Fontaine, *Traditional Sayings in the Old Testament* (Sheffield, U.K.: Almond, 1982), p. 50.

[2]I found Daniel J. Estes, *Hear, My Son: Teaching and Learning in Proverbs 1-9* (Grand Rapids, Mich.: Eerdmans, 1998), pp. 87-100, very helpful in this area.

[3]The NKJV mistakes *Sheol* for hell rather than "the grave." The proverb teaches that an undisciplined child may well engage in behavior that will send him to an early grave.

Chapter 6: Did Solomon Know Amenemope and Ahiqar?

[1] See the relationship between Proverbs 22:17-24:22 and the *Instructions of Amenemope*.

[2]Edmund I. Gordon, *Sumerian Proverbs: Glimpses of Everyday Life in Ancient Mesopotamia* (Philadelphia: The University Museum, 1959), and more recently, Bendt Alster, *Proverbs of Ancient Sumer*, 2 vols. (Bethesda, Md.: CDL Press, 1997).

[3]The translations as well as the numbering of the Sumerian proverbs comes from Alster.

[4]Alster, *Proverbs of Ancient Sumer*, p. xviii.

[5]Translations of the Instructions of Shuruppak are also from Alster, but can also be found in *Context of Scripture*, 1:569-70.

[6]See ANET, pp. 425-27. A more recent translation of the Counsels of Wisdom may be found in Benjamin Foster, *Before the Muses* (Potomac, Md.: CDL Press, 1996), pp. 328-31. There is also a text from Ugarit, written in Akkadian, that is the advice of a man named Shube-

Awilim to his son (Foster, *Before the Muses*, pp. 332-35).
[7]See his comments in W. G. Lambert, *Babylonian Wisdom Literature* (Oxford: Clarendon, 1960).
[8]J. D. Ray, "Egyptian Wisdom Literature," in *Wisdom in Ancient Israel*, ed. J. Day et al. (Cambridge: Cambridge University Press, 1995), p. 18, notes this but suggests that "enlightenment" may be closer to its true meaning.
[9]The oldest extant Instruction is the *Instruction of Hardjedef*.
[10]Miriam Lichtheim, *Ancient Egyptian Literature* (Berkeley: University of California Press, 1975), 1:97.
[11]John Ruffle, "The Teaching of Amenemope and Its Connection with the Book of Proverbs," *Tyndale Bulletin* 28 (1977): 33. See R. J. Williams, "The Alleged Semitic Original for the Wisdom of Amenemope," *Journal of Egyptian Archaeology* 47 (1961): 106; B. Peterson, *Studia Aegyptiaca* 1 (1974): 323-27; Paul Overland, "Structure in *The Wisdom of Amenemope* and Proverbs," in *"Go the Land I Will Show You,"* ed. J. E. Coleson and Victor H. Matthews (Winona Lake, Ind.: Eisenbrauns, 1996), pp. 275-91.
[12]All translations of this text are from J. A. Wilson, *ANET*, pp. 421-25.
[13]Wilson, *ANET*, p. 421.
[14]The text may be found in Lichtheim, *Ancient Egyptian Literature*, 3:159-84.
[15]J. D. Ray, "Egyptian Wisdom Literature," p. 26.
[16]Translation from M. Lichtheim, *Ancient Egyptian Literature* (Berkeley: University of California Press, 1980), 3:171.
[17]The most definitive edition of this text, and the translation that I cite here, is in James Lindenberger, *The Aramaic Proverbs of Ahiqar* (Baltimore: Johns Hopkins University Press, 1983).
[18]Richard J. Clifford, *Proverbs* (Louisville, Ky.: Westminster John Knox, 1999), p. 8.
[19]These examples (including the translation of Amenemope) are taken from Ruffle, "Teaching of Amenemope," pp. 29-68.
[20]Alfred Erman, *Sitzungsberichte der Prussischen Akademie der Wissenschaften* in 1924.
[21]Robert O. Kevin, *The Wisdom of Amen-em-ope and Its Possible Dependence on the Book of Proverbs* (Austria: Adolf Mozhausen's Successors, 1931).
[22]The NLT does register its opinion that this is speculative by adding a footnote to "thirty sayings" that reads "Or *excellent sayings*; the meaning of the Hebrew is uncertain."
[23]Quoted in Clifford, *Proverbs*, p. 12.
[24]Translation from Lichtheim, *Ancient Egyptian Literature*, 2:136-37.
[25]Translations are from John Day, "Foreign Semitic Influence on the Wisdom of Israel," in *Wisdom in Ancient Israel* (Cambridge: Cambridge University Press, 1995), p. 64,

Chapter 7: Proverbs in Conversation with Job and Ecclesiastes
[1]For further details, see Tremper Longman III, *Ecclesiastes*, NICOT (Grand Rapids, Mich.: Eerdmans, 1997).
[2]The term is Bruce Waltke's. See his "Does Proverbs Promise Too Much?" *Andrews University Seminary Studies* 34 (1996): 319-26, and the earlier article by Raymond van Leeuwen, "Wealth and Poverty: System and Contradiction in Proverbs," *Hebrew Studies* 33 (1992): 25-36. See the better-than proverbs of 15:16-17; 16:8, 19; 17:1; 19:22b; 22:1; 28:6, as well as 10:2; 11:15; 13:23; 14:31; 15:25; 18:23; 21:6, 7, 13; 19:10; 22:8, 22; 23:17; 28:15-16, 27.
[3]However, Waltke makes the case too optimistically. I do not accept all aspects of his argument, particularly his philological comments on the word *hayyim* (p. 328).

Chapter 8: Proverbial Wisdom in Action: Joseph and Daniel

James L. Crenshaw. "Method in Determining Wisdom Influence upon 'Historical' Literature," *Journal of Biblical Literature* 88 (1969): 129-42. See more recently, Michael V. Fox, "Wisdom in the Joseph Story," *Vetus Testamentum* 51 (2001): 26-41.

[2]Genesis 38, the story of Judah and Tamar, seems on the surface to interrupt the narrative flow of the Joseph story, and in a sense, it does. However, this concluding section of Genesis is really about Jacob's sons, so stories about two of those sons dominate.

[3]Benjamin is born at a later point in the narrative.

[4]Unfortunately, we cannot explore the entire book or even the first half of it in any detail. Interested readers may consult Tremper Longman III, *Daniel*, NIVAC (Grand Rapids, Mich.: Zondervan, 1999).

[5]For instance, note that in Daniel 10:3 the text implies that Daniel had gone back to eating the king's rich food.

[6]Again, for more on this, consult Longman, *Daniel*, pp. 51-54.

[7]Daniel is no schemer in our story, because he does not have a malicious intent. The latter separates scheming from wise planning.

[8]A. Leo Oppenheim, *The Interpretation of Dreams in the Ancient Near East* (Philadelphia: American Philosophical Society, 1956).

[9]For this, see Longman, *Daniel*, pp. 79-83.

Chapter 9: Where Is God in Proverbs?

[1]Based on Akkadian cognate *ummanu*; other suggestions include "nursling"; cf. Michael V. Fox, *Proverbs 1-9*, Anchor Bible (Garden City, N.Y.: Doubleday, 2000), pp. 285-86.

[2]See the NLT footnote.

Chapter 10: How to Study Themes in Proverbs

[1]See the full extent of the evidence given in Daniel C. Snell, *Twice-Told Proverbs* (Winona Lake, Ind.: Eisenbrauns, 1993).

[2]This is not the place to develop it, but I am not persuaded by the recent tendency to find deep structures of organization in the book of Proverbs. A recent example, which includes a review of other attempts to find structure, is K. Heim, *Like Grapes of Gold Set in Silver: An Interpretation of Proverbial Clusters in Proverbs 10:1—22:16* (Berlin: Walter de Gruyter, 2001).

[3]This important subject has been treated before by scholars, and even though I do not agree with everything they say on the subject, I want to acknowledge the stimulation I received by reading R. N. Whybray, *Wealth and Poverty in the Book of Proverbs* (Sheffield, U.K.: JSOT Press, 1990), and Harold C. Washington, *Wealth and Poverty in the Instruction of Amenemope and the Book of Proverbs*, SBLDS 142 (Atlanta: Scholars Press, 1993).

Chapter 11: On Loving the Right Woman

[1]For a detailed interpretation as well as a close look at the ancient Near Eastern background, see Tremper Longman III, *The Book of Song of Songs* (Grand Rapids, Mich.: Eerdmans, 2001).

[2]See Robin Wakely in her article on *hayil* in *New International Dictionary of Old Testament Theology and Exegesis*, ed. William A. VanGemeren (Grand Rapids, Mich.: Zondervan, 1997), 2:118.

Chapter 12: Wise Words, Foolish Words

[1]The bracketed words are in the Hebrew but not represented in the NLT translation.

[2]See Kevin Vanhoozer, *Is There a Meaning in This Text? The Bible, the Reader, and the Morality of Literary Knowledge* (Grand Rapids, Mich.: Zondervan, 1998).

Appendix 1: Authorship and Date of the Book of Proverbs

[1]Gleason Archer, *A Survey of Old Testament Introduction* (Chicago: Moody Press, 1964), pp. 476-77.

[2]C. H. Toy, *The Book of Proverbs* (New York: Scribner's, 1916), pp. xix-xx. Indeed, it is not uncommon today to come across scholars who argue that Solomon (not to speak of David and the United Monarchy) was a fictional creation of a group of people living in the Persian or Hellenistic period.

[3]J. Alberto Soggin, *Introduction to the Old Testament* (Philadelphia: Westminster Press, 1976), p. 384.

[4]Presented most forcefully in William McKane, *Proverbs: A New Approach,* Old Testament Library (Philadelphia: Westminster Press, 1970).

[5]Gerhard von Rad, *Wisdom in Israel* (Nashville: Abingdon, 1972), pp., 24-50.

[6]In Christa Kayatz, *Studien zu israelitischen Spruchweisheit,* WMANT 28 (Neukirchen Vluyn, Germany: Neukirchener Verlag, 1968).

Author Index

Subject Index

Scripture Index